INDOOR GRILLING RECIPES

Eric Theiss

POWER
SMOKELESS GRILL™

First Edition

Published by Tristar Products, Inc.

Printed in China.

PSG_COOKBOOK_TP_ENG_V1_180801

ACKNOWLEDGMENTS

I feel incredibly lucky to have had so many talented people help me to bring this book to fruition. I depend on Claire Winslow not only for her vast culinary knowledge and attention to detail but also for her ability to keep me on task. I would also like to acknowledge the hard work put in by her team, including Andrew Bergman and Ed Buldowski. Thank you to Jeanette Mostowicz for her food styling contributions and ability to put up with me. Thanks to Skippy Sicari for his numerous contributions as the Prime Minister of Props and as my stunt double!

For making the book look beautiful with its art and design, I would be remiss if I didn't thank Parker Bliss and Daniel Suquitana. To my photographer Matt Wagemann and his assistant Mike Livi, thank you for getting great shots of me despite my lack of modeling skills and for making the food pop off of the page so well. Also, big thanks to Pete Calciano for bringing all of these talented people together and for being so accommodating.

Lastly, I would like to thank Elizabeth Jones and Joann Herrera for powdering, poking, and prodding until I look good enough for the camera. Now THAT takes a village.

Eric Theiss

TABLE OF CONTENTS

APPETIZERS

SALADS

SANDWICHES

QUESADILLAS

PIZZA

CHICKEN

FISH & SEAFOOD

MEATS

VEGGIES

DESSERTS

ABOUT THE AUTHOR

Eric Theiss's culinary savoir-faire started in northern New Jersey as a child when his Italian mother, on a hunch, borrowed his first cookbook from the public library at age 6. His mother was right, and Eric began a life of culinary work. As a young adult, he continued to fuel his passion for food and fine dining. During his early twenties, his love of food and wine manifested itself in working long nights in NJ restaurants, including his favorite kitchen of all, Culinary Renaissance, where acclaimed chef Frank Falcinelli (owner of NY coffee shop Cafe Pedlar and restaurants Frankies 457 Spuntino, Frankies 570 Spuntino, and Prime Meats) exposed Eric to a level of culinary passion that inspired him to strive. In 1997, he took a leap of faith and opened his own fine dining restaurant and bar, Meritage, in West Chester, PA--which enjoyed rave reviews from some prominent Philadelphia food critics. There, his dream of owning and operating a fine dining establishment was fully realized.

A few years later, utilizing his inventive and creative flair, Eric moved on to the culinary broadcast world, working not only in product development for QVC's proprietary kitchenware lines, but also for celebrity lines (Paula Deen, Emeril, Rocco, Rachel Ray) as well as his own personal line of cool kitchen tools and cookware, Walah!. Eric has been a popular regular TV Chef presenter for over 15 years on QVC's live shows for his own brands as well as a variety of well-known national kitchen brands. Beyond that, Eric owns and operates a company that brokers many new and innovative products into QVC. His most recent business venture, a successful publishing company (also named Walah!), publishes and distributes cookbooks and pamphlets nationwide.

Paramount to his career thus far, Eric currently hosts several incredibly successful, award-winning infomercials featuring the Power Pressure Cooker XL, the Power Air Fryer Oven and the Copper Chef, each of which has sold millions of units and achieved award-winning accolades and top of the charts. Eric wrote this cookbook to complement his newest infomercial, the Power Smokeless Grill, which gives people the opportunity to grill/griddle indoors, virtually smoke free!

Eric currently resides near the live studios of QVC in PA along with his wife, Jessica and his two sons, Cameron and Maxwell.

QUESTIONS & ANSWERS

1. Where can I use the Power Smokeless Grill?

The Power Smokeless Grill is designed to cook authentic, char-grilled BBQ meals indoors all year round. On any day in any weather!

2. How does the Power Smokeless Grill help keep my kitchen clean?

The Power Smokeless Grill includes a stainless, tempered glass to help keep your countertop clean while Turbo-Speed Smoke Extractor Technology helps keep your kitchen virtually smoke-less.

3. Are the parts included easy to clean?

Yes! The Grill and Griddle Plates are designed with Advanced Nonstick Coating, so nothing sticks to the surface. There's no soaking or scrubbing required afterwards. Both the Grill & Griddle Plates are dishwasher safe or you may wash by hand.

4. How much can I cook on the Power Smokeless Grill?

The Power Smokeless Grill has an extra large 13.75" x 8" grilling surface. You can grill six burgers or four steaks at one time.

5. What are the dimensions of the Power Smokeless Grill?

The Power Smokeless Grill measures 19.7" L x 11.4" W x. 7.5" H with lid and 19.7" L X 11.4" W X 5.1" H without lid.

6. How does the Power Smokeless Grill transform into an electric skillet?

You can turn the Power Smokeless Grill into an electric skillet in seconds by replacing the Grill Plate with the Griddle Plate.

7. How does the Power Smokeless Grill help me cook healthier?

When cooking on the Power Smokeless Grill, fat and oil drain away into the removable Drip Tray. Plus, Advanced Nonstick Coating means no added butter or oil is required.

8. How do I control the cooking temperature on the Power Smokeless Grill?

The Power Smokeless Grill's LED Smart Temperature Control lets you adjust the temperature from 220° F to 450° F with just the push of a button. Heat is distributed evenly for perfect grilling without hot spots.

9. How does the Power Smokeless Grill reduce virtually all the smoke from grilling?

The Power Smokeless Grill's Turbo-Speed Smoke Extractor Technology sucks up smoke and odor utilizing a smoke recycling system. The smoke is captured and extracted through an advanced fan system, greatly reducing the amount of smoke that is let out.

10. What type of utensils should I use?

In order to preserve the nonstick surface, we recommend you use only nonmetallic utensils made of wood, plastic, silicone, or bamboo.

WHY POWER SMOKELESS GRILL?

We all love the idea of grilling our food for that juicy, char-grilled flavor and texture, but not all of us love the idea of having to go outside to do it. Often the weather doesn't cooperate, plus there is all of that unpleasant smoke and odor as well as nasty flare-ups! Now we offer you an amazing option for grilling…INDOORS! The Power Smokeless Grill solves all of the problems associated with outdoor grilling and allows you to grill right in the comfort of your home, apartment, patio, boat or RV!

The Power Smokeless Grill contains new technology that extracts virtually all of the smoke from its source and sucks it away so that neither you nor

your smoke detector will detect smoke! It's so convenient to grill and get delicious real grill marks and char-grilled flavor indoors on our amazing heavy duty cast aluminum plate with the heat source built into it. It's encased in high-end ceramic nonstick, which makes clean up a joke, and all parts except for the electrical base unit are dishwasher safe! This means that the drippings and grease can slip right down underneath into a collection tray, unlike on your grill where grease falls right into the heat source and causes flare-ups that ruin your expensive meat and seafood!

Not only can you grill indoors, but our temperature dial allows you to cook in many other ways, too. You can slow-grill foods like wings and pizzas at 350° F, or melt paninis and other cheesy delights at 300° F, or even steam seafood and veggies in the Griddle Plate using the included lid. Plus, the Griddle Plate gives you the versatility to use it everyday for everything you cook from eggs to pancakes to stir fry and cheesesteaks. It's small enough to take up little room in your kitchen, but large enough to feed a hungry family!

EQUIVALENCY CHARTS

Dry (Weight) Measurements

Misc.*	Teaspoons	Tablespoons	Ounces	Cups	Grams	Pounds
1 dash	$1/16$ tsp.	-	-	-	-	-
1 pinch/6 drops	$1/8$ tsp.	-	-	-	-	-
15 drops	¼ tsp.	-	-	-	-	-
1 splash	½ tsp.	-	-	-	-	-
-	1 tsp.	$1/3$ tbsp.	$1/6$ oz	-	-	-
-	3 tsp.	1 tbsp.	½ oz	-	14.3 g	-
-	-	2 tbsp.	1 oz	$1/8$ cup	28.3 g	-
-	-	4 tbsp.	2 oz	¼ cup	56.7 g	-
-	-	5 $1/3$ tbsp.	2.6 oz	$1/3$ cup	75.6 g	-
-	-	8 tbsp.	4 oz	½ cup	113.4 g	-
-	-	12 tbsp.	6 oz	¾ cup	170.1 g	-
-	-	16 tbsp.	8 oz	1 cup	226.8 g	½ lb
-	-	32 tbsp.	16 oz	2 cups	453.6 g	1 lb
-	-	64 tbsp.	32 oz	4 cups/1 qt.	907.2 g	2 lb

* Dash, pinch, drop, and splash are subjective measurements that have no formally agreed-upon definition.

Abbreviations

Term	Dry & Liquid	Abbreviation
cup	usually liquid	-
fluid ounce	only liquid	fl oz.
gallon	dry or liquid	-
inch	-	in.
ounce	dry	oz.
pint	dry or liquid	-
pound	dry	lb
quart	dry or liquid	qt./qts.
teaspoon	dry or liquid	tsp.
tablespoon	dry or liquid	tbsp.

Liquid (Volume) Measurements

Fluid Ounces	Tablespoons	Cups	Milliliter/Liters	Pints	Quarts	Gallons
1 fl oz	2 tbsp.	1/8 cup	30 ml	-	-	-
2 fl oz	4 tbsp.	1/4 cup	60 ml	-	-	-
4 fl oz	8 tbsp.	1/2 cup	125 ml	-	-	-
8 fl oz	16 tbsp.	1 cup	250 ml	-	-	-
12 fl oz	-	1 1/2 cups	375 ml	-	-	-
16 fl oz	-	2 cups	500 ml	1 pint	-	-
32 fl oz	-	4 cups	1 L	2 pints	1 qt.	-
128 fl oz	-	16 cups	4 L	8 pints	4 qts.	1 gallon

COOKING TEMPERATURE CHARTS

Safe steps in food handling, cooking, and storage are essential for preventing foodborne illness. You can't see, smell, or taste harmful bacteria that may cause illness.

Cook all food to these minimum internal temperatures as measured with a food thermometer before removing food from the heat source. Let rest for a minimum of 10 mins. before serving unless indicated otherwise.

In every step of food preparation, follow the four guidelines to help keep food safe:

Clean—*Wash hands and surfaces often.*
Separate—*Separate raw meat from other foods.*
Cook—*Cook to the right temperature.*
Chill—*Refrigerate food promptly.*

Doneness	Serving Temperature	Serving Temperature
	Eric's Recommendation	**USDA's Recommendation**
Beef, Lamb, Pork, Veal Steaks, Chops & Roasts		
Rare	125° F (52° C)	*
Medium Rare	130° F (54° C)	*
Medium	135° F (57° C)	
Medium Well	150° F (65° C)	Minimum Internal Temperature & Rest Time: 145° F (63° C) and allow to rest for at least 3 mins.*
Well Done	Over 150° F (over 65° C)	

Doneness	Serving Temperature	Serving Temperature
	Eric's Recommendation	**USDA's Recommendation**
Ground Meats, Burgers, Meatloaf & Sausages Except Poultry		
Recommended	160° F (71° C)	Minimum Internal Temperature: 160° F (71° C)*
Burgers (Beef)		
Recommended	140° F (60° C)	160° F (71° C)
Pork Ribs, Pork Shoulders		
Tender and Juicy	180-190° F (82–88° C)	*
Precooked Ham		
Recommended	140° F (60° C)	Reheat cooked hams packaged in USDA-inspected plants to 140° F (60° C); all others to 165° F (74° C)*
Turkey & Chicken, Whole or Ground		
Recommended	165° F (74° C)	Minimum Internal Temperature: 165° F (74° C)*
Fish		
Rare	125° F (52° C)	*
Medium	135° F (57° C)	*
Well Done	145° F (63° C)	Minimum Internal Temperature: 145° F (63° C)*
Unpasteurized Eggs		
Recommended	160° F (71° C)	Minimum Internal Temperature: 160° F (71° C)*

*Consuming raw or undercooked meats, poultry, seafood, shellfish, or eggs may increase your risk of foodborne illness.
http://fsis.usda.gov/

ERIC'S FAVORITE RUBS

I like to make these rubs and store them in small **air-tight containers**. These recipes **yield about a ½ cup**. Making extra rubs saves time and money, and you will definitely enjoy having some versatile flavors at the ready in your cooking arsenal. Use these rubs not just for meat, fish and poultry; you can also sprinkle the Everyday Rub on a salad for some extra punch. Try the Poultry Rub on grilled veggies. The Red Meat Rub is great for flavoring your meatloaf mix. The idea is to play around and see how many different things you can do with them!

Directions: *Mix all of the ingredients together until well incorporated. You can make into a fine powder by placing into a blender or spice grinder.*

Poultry

2 tbsp. crushed sea salt

2 tbsp. paprika

1 tsp. sugar

1 tbsp. turmeric

2 tsp. garlic powder

2 tsp. granulated dried onion

1 tbsp. ground thyme

1 tsp. mustard powder

½ tsp. cayenne

2 tsp. dried lemon peel

1 tbsp. ground black pepper

Everyday

2 tbsp. crushed sea salt

2 tbsp. crushed black pepper

2 tbsp. granulated garlic

2 tbsp. granulated onion

1 tbsp. dried basil

½ tsp. red pepper flakes

1 tbsp. coriander

1 tsp. dry mustard

1 tsp. brown sugar

Fish

1 tbsp. crushed sea salt

1 tbsp. onion powder

1 tsp. thyme

2 tsp. tarragon

1 tbsp. dried parsley

1 tbsp. dried chives

1 tbsp. ground white pepper

1 tbsp. dried lemon peel

1 tsp. celery seed

Red Meat

2 tbsp. crushed sea salt

2 tbsp. brown sugar

2 tbsp. ground black coffee

1 tbsp. granulated garlic

1 tbsp. granulated onion

1 tbsp. cumin

1 tbsp. coriander

1 tbsp. ground black pepper

APPETIZERS

Grilled Stuffed Portobello Mushrooms

SERVES 2

Ingredients

Spinach Stuffing

2 large portobello mushrooms, with stems

2 tbsp. olive oil

1 clove garlic, peeled & minced

3 cups spinach

---

2 plum tomatoes, chopped

½ cup shredded mozzarella cheese

2 tbsp. shredded Parmesan cheese

2 tbsp. panko breadcrumbs

½ cup bacon, cooked crisp & chopped

Directions

1. Place the Grill Plate on the Power Smokeless Grill and preheat Grill to 350° F.

2. Separate mushroom stems from caps and finely chop the stems. Reserve caps.

3. Heat olive oil in a sauté pan on the stove top. Add garlic and cook over medium-high heat for 3 mins. Add mushroom stems and spinach and cook until tender. Remove from the heat and set aside.

4. Place the mushroom caps on the Grill Plate. Fill each cap with spinach stuffing, top with tomatoes, and cook to desired doneness. Remove mushrooms.

5. Preheat the broiler.

6. Sprinkle mozzarella, Parmesan, and breadcrumbs over mushrooms.

7. Broil mushrooms until breadcrumbs are toasted and cheese is melted.

8. Top the mushrooms with the bacon.

Eric's Tip: I love to turn these into an Eggs Benedict-style dish by topping with a poached egg.

Cheese-Stuffed Dates

Ingredients

¼ cup bleu cheese, crumbled

¼ cup cream cheese

_____

20 dates, pitted

10 slices bacon, raw, cut in half

Directions

1. Place the Grill Plate on the Power Smokeless Grill and preheat the Grill to 350° F.

2. Preheat the oven to 390° F.

3. In a medium bowl, stir together bleu cheese and cream cheese.

4. Cut a slit (lengthwise) into each date.

5. Stuff each date with a spoonful of cheese stuffing.

6. Roll a bacon slice half around each date.

7. Place the dates on the Grill Plate and grill 2–3 mins. per side.

8. Transfer to the oven and cook until bacon is crispy (8–10 mins.).

Eric's Tip: I'll add a shelled pistachio or walnut into each date for an extra crunch.

Korean Beef Skewers

Ingredients

Marinade

½ cup soy sauce

1 tbsp. rice vinegar

¼ cup brown sugar

2 tbsp. sesame oil

2 cloves garlic, peeled & minced

4 scallions, sliced

---

1 lb beef flank steak, cut into strips

1 tsp. sesame seeds

1 tsp. crushed red pepper

Directions

1. Combine the marinade ingredients in a large bowl.

2. Add steak to marinade, cover, and marinate for 2 hrs. in the refrigerator.

3. Place the Grill Plate on the Power Smokeless Grill and preheat the Grill to 390° F.

4. Skewer the steak, place on the Grill Plate, and grill each side to desired doneness.

5. Sprinkle with sesame seeds and crushed red pepper to serve.

Eric's Tip: Serve with some jasmine rice and bibb lettuce for delicious wraps.

Chicken Satay

Ingredients

Peanut Sauce

1 cup peanut butter

2 tbsp. minced shallots

2 tbsp. brown sugar

½ tsp. curry powder

1 tbsp. soy sauce

1 tbsp. mirin rice wine

juice of 1 lime

1 clove garlic, peeled & minced

---

2 small chicken breasts, thinly sliced

½ cup chopped peanuts

2 scallions, sliced

Directions

1. In a large bowl, stir together peanut sauce ingredients.

2. Marinate the chicken breasts in the peanut sauce for 4 hrs. in the refrigerator.

3. Place the Grill Plate on the Power Smokeless Grill and preheat the Grill to 390° F.

4. Skewer the chicken breasts, place skewers on the Grill Plate, and cook each side until cooked through (5–7 mins. per side).

5. Top the skewers with the peanuts and scallions.

Eric's Tip: I love to substitute the chicken for shrimp then toss them with chilled sesame noodles.

Mozzarella Crostini & Grilled Tomatoes

Ingredients

Olive Oil Marinade

½ cup extra virgin olive oil

2 cloves garlic, peeled & minced

1 tsp. dried oregano

½ tsp. sea salt

½ tsp. ground black pepper

½ crusty baguette, sliced into ½-inch rounds

1 cup grape tomatoes

12 slices fresh mozzarella cheese

2 tbsp. balsamic glaze

3 basil leaves, chopped, for garnish

Directions

1. Place the Grill Plate on the Power Smokeless Grill and preheat the Grill to 350° F.

2. Combine the olive oil marinade ingredients in a bowl.

3. Brush both sides of each baguette slice with marinade.

4. Place the baguette slices on the Grill Plate, and grill each side until toasted. Remove and set aside.

5. Toss the tomatoes in the remaining olive oil marinade.

6. Place the tomatoes on the Grill Plate, and grill to desired doneness.

7. Top each baguette slice with 1 slice mozzarella cheese and a spoonful of tomatoes.

8. Drizzle balsamic glaze and remaining marinade over crostini.

9. Garnish with basil.

Eric's Tip: If you can't find nice ripe tomatoes, grill some zucchini and top with chopped sun-dried tomato.

Grilled Peach & Pineapple Salsa

Ingredients

2 peaches, halved, pitted

1 cup sliced pineapple

½ red onion, sliced into rings

½ red pepper, sliced into strips

2 tbsp. chopped cilantro

1 tbsp. lime juice

½ jalapeño, minced

1 tsp. sugar

½ tsp. sea salt

blue corn tortilla chips, for serving

Directions

1. Place the Grill Plate on the Power Smokeless Grill and preheat the Grill to 350° F.

2. Place the peaches, pineapple, red onion, and red pepper on the Grill Plate and cook on all sides.

3. Remove, cool slightly and dice.

4. In a large bowl, combine diced peaches, pineapple, red onion, and red pepper with the cilantro, lime juice, jalapeño, sugar, and salt.

5. Serve salsa with the tortilla chips.

Eric's Tip: If there is any left over, I like to add it to my Jasmine rice for a delicious island-style side dish.

31

Mushroom Bruschetta

Ingredients

1 baguette, split

¼ cup extra virgin olive oil

2 cloves garlic, peeled

8 slices mozzarella cheese

6 portobello mushrooms

¼ cup olive oil

2 sprigs rosemary, chopped

1 tsp. sea salt

1 tbsp. balsamic glaze

1 tbsp. chopped parsley

Directions

1. Place the Grill Plate on the Power Smokeless Grill and preheat the Grill to 350° F.

2. Brush the baguette with the extra virgin olive oil.

3. Place the baguette on the Grill Plate and cook each side until toasted. Remove.

4. Rub baguette with garlic and top with the mozzarella cheese. Set aside.

5. Combine the mushrooms, olive oil, rosemary, and sea salt in a bowl.

6. Place the mushrooms on the Grill Plate and cook until tender. Remove and cool slightly.

7. Thinly slice mushrooms and layer over prepared baguette.

8. To serve, drizzle balsamic glaze and sprinkle parsley over bruschetta.

Eric's Tip: Cremini mushrooms are just baby portobellos so you can swap them out if you wish.

Cheese-Stuffed Sweet Mini Peppers

Ingredients

8 oz cream cheese, softened

½ cup chopped pepperoni

⅔ cup shredded Asiago cheese

⅔ cup shredded mozzarella cheese

---

2 tbsp. chopped basil

12 mini peppers, cut in half
& seeded

2 scallions, sliced, for garnish

Directions

1. Place the Grill Plate on the Power Smokeless Grill and preheat the Grill to 350° F.

2. Preheat the oven to 350° F.

3. In a medium bowl, stir together the cream cheese filling ingredients.

4. Stuff each pepper with filling.

5. Place the peppers on the Grill Plate, cover with the glass lid, and cook until tender.

6. Transfer to the oven to finish until cooked through and bubbly (5–10 mins.).

7. Sprinkle the scallions over the peppers.

Eric's Tip: Wrap the peppers in bacon for awesome poppers!

Maryland Crab Cakes

Ingredients

Crab Cake Mixture

1 lb lump crab meat

1 egg

¾ cup soda crackers, crushed

1 tbsp. Dijon mustard

1 tsp. seafood seasoning

1 shallot, peeled & minced

¼ cup mayonnaise

½ tsp. ground black pepper

1 red pepper, diced small

---

2 tbsp. canola oil

tartar sauce, for serving

lemon wedges, for serving

Directions

1. Place the Griddle Plate on the Power Smokeless Grill and preheat the Grill to 390° F.

2. In a large bowl, mix together the crab cake mixture ingredients.

3. Form the crab cake mixture into 4 3-oz cakes.

4. Heat the canola oil on the Griddle Plate. Once the oil is heated, add the crab cakes and cook both sides until golden and cooked through (5–7 mins. per side).

5. Serve with the tartar sauce and lemon wedges.

Griddle Recipe

Eggs in a Basket

SERVES 4

Ingredients

4 slices white bread

¼ cup margarine

4 eggs

½ cup shredded cheddar cheese

sea salt & ground black pepper, to serve

Directions

1. Place the Griddle Plate on the Power Smokeless Grill and preheat the Grill to 320° F.

2. Spread margarine onto one side of each bread slice.

3. Cut a hole into the center of each bread slice.

4. Place the bread slices (margarine side-down) on the Griddle Plate. Crack an egg into the center of each bread slice and top with cheddar cheese.

5. Cook for 3–5 mins per side.

6. Season with salt and ground black pepper.

Griddle Recipe

Chive, Avocado & Goat Cheese Omelet

SERVES 1

Ingredients

3 egg whites, beaten

1 tbsp. chopped chives

¼ tsp. sea salt

¼ tsp. ground black pepper

1 tbsp. grapeseed oil

2 tbsp. crumbled goat cheese

½ avocado, sliced

Directions

1. Place the Griddle Plate on the Power Smokeless Grill and preheat the Grill to 390° F for 3–5 mins.

2. Whisk together the egg whites, chives, salt, and ground black pepper.

3. Heat the grapeseed oil on the Griddle Plate. Once hot, add the egg white mixture. Sprinkle the goat cheese and avocado over the egg whites, and cook to desired doneness.

4. Fold the omelet before plating.

Griddle Recipe

Grilled Chicken
& Pineapple Salad

Grilled Chipotle Chicken Salad

Grilled Shrimp Caesar Salad

Warm Tomato Caprese

Grilled Scallops with Green
Goddess Dressing

Grilled Watermelon Salad

Grilled Corn Salad

Arugula Salad with Grilled
Tomato Vinaigrette

Grilled Bread Salad

SALADS

Grilled Chicken & Pineapple Salad

SERVES 2

Ingredients

Marinade

3 tbsp. olive oil

1 tsp. sea salt

½ tsp. ground black pepper

½ tsp. onion powder

½ tsp. garlic powder

½ tsp. paprika

2 tbsp. red wine vinegar

———————

¼ pineapple, trimmed & cut into wedges

2 small chicken breasts

Dressing

juice of ½ lemon

¼ cup extra virgin olive oil

½ tsp. sea salt

½ tsp. ground black pepper

1 tsp. honey

———————

3 cups kale

1 cup cooked quinoa

Directions

1. Combine the marinade ingredients in a bowl. Add chicken, toss to coat and marinate for 1 hr. in the refrigerator.

2. Place the Grill Plate on the Power Smokeless Grill and preheat the Grill to 390° F.

3. Place the pineapple on the Grill Plate and cook on each side until tender. Remove and reserve.

4. Place the chicken breasts on the Grill and cook for 6–7 mins. per side, or until cooked through and registering 165° F. Allow chicken to rest.

5. Combine the dressing ingredients in a bowl.

6. Toss kale and quinoa with the dressing and top with grilled pineapple.

7. Slice chicken and serve with the salad.

Eric's Tip: I love to add feta cheese then roll it up in a tortilla for a killer burrito!

Grilled Chipotle Chicken Salad

Ingredients

Marinade

2 chipotle peppers, minced

1 clove garlic, peeled & minced

½ tsp. sea salt

½ tsp. ground coriander

2 tbsp. olive oil

juice of ½ lime

---

2 small chicken breasts

Dressing

¼ cup buttermilk

1 tbsp. Worcestershire sauce

½ tsp. garlic powder

½ tsp. onion powder

½ tsp. sea salt

½ tsp. ground black pepper

½ tsp. Dijon mustard

1 tsp. sugar

Salad

4 cups chopped romaine lettuce

½ cup grape tomatoes, halved

½ red onion, peeled & sliced

½ cucumber, sliced

Directions

1. Combine the marinade ingredients in a bowl, add chicken and toss to coat.

2. Marinate for 1 hr. in the refrigerator.

3. Place the Grill Plate on the Power Smokeless Grill and preheat the Grill to 390° F.

4. Place chicken breasts on the Grill and cook 6–7 mins. per side, until cooked through and registering 165° F. Allow chicken to rest.

5. Combine the dressing ingredients.

6. Combine the salad ingredients and toss with the dressing.

7. Slice chicken and serve with the salad.

Eric's Tip: I love to get pre-made pizza dough, roll it thin, then grill it for the best salad pizza.

Ingredients

Caesar Dressing

2 egg yolks

6 anchovies

1 clove garlic, peeled

juice of 1 lemon, divided

½ cup olive oil, divided

1 tbsp. mustard

½ tsp. Worcestershire sauce

salt, to taste

ground black pepper, to taste

Croutons

1 cup cubed baguette

½ tbsp. garlic powder

½ tsp. sea salt

2 tbsp. olive oil

Shrimp Marinade

2 tbsp. olive oil

1 tsp. sea salt

1 tsp. ground black pepper

1 tbsp. lemon juice

12 16–20 shrimp, peeled
& deveined

1 head romaine lettuce, chopped

¼ cup grated Parmesan cheese

Grilled Shrimp Caesar Salad

Directions

1. Combine the egg yolks, anchovies, garlic, and 1 tbsp. lemon juice in a food processor.

2. Drizzle in ¼ cup olive oil very slowly.

3. Add mustard, Worcestershire sauce, remaining olive oil and lemon juice, and season with salt and ground black pepper.

4. Place the Grill Plate on the Power Smokeless Grill and preheat the Grill to 390° F.

5. Combine the croutons ingredients in a bowl and toss.

6. Place the croutons on the Grill Plate and grill until charred and toasted. Remove to cool.

7. Combine the shrimp marinade ingredients in a bowl and add shrimp to coat.

8. Place shrimp on the Grill Plate and grill 3–5 mins. per side, until cooked through. Remove and reserve.

9. Combine lettuce, croutons, and ½ cup Caesar dressing and toss gently.

10. Divide salad between two plates, top each with 6 shrimp, and sprinkle with Parmesan.

Eric's Tip: Salmon or tuna fillets work well with this dish too!

Warm Tomato Caprese

Ingredients

1 eggplant, sliced into ¼ in. thick rounds

1 tsp. sea salt

½ tsp. ground black pepper

1 clove garlic, peeled & minced

6 tbsp. extra virgin olive oil, divided

1 lb mozzarella cheese, sliced

3 beefsteak tomatoes, sliced ½ in. thick

1 tbsp. balsamic glaze

1 tbsp. basil pesto

2 tbsp. pea tendrils

Directions

1. Place the Grill Plate on the Power Smokeless Grill and preheat the Grill to 350° F.

2. Combine the eggplant, salt, ground black pepper, garlic, and 4 tbsp. extra virgin olive oil in a bowl and toss to coat.

3. Place eggplant on the Grill Plate and grill until tender (3–5 mins. per side).

4. Layer and stack the eggplant, mozzarella and tomato evenly between four plates to make towers.

5. Drizzle evenly with balsamic glaze and remaining 2 tbsp. extra virgin olive oil.

6. Just before serving, top with pesto and pea tendrils.

Eric's Tip: Turn this into a party appetizer by shingling the tomato and grilled eggplant around burrata mozzarella.

Grilled Scallops with Green Goddess Dressing

Ingredients

Green Goddess Dressing

3 anchovies

3 tbsp. minced chives

¾ cup parsley

¼ cup tarragon

1 clove garlic, peeled & chopped

1 cup mayonnaise

1 cup sour cream

2 tbsp. lemon juice

1 tsp. sea salt

½ tsp. ground black pepper

Scallop Marinade

¼ cup olive oil

½ tsp. sea salt

½ tbsp. ground black pepper

1 lb large scallops

2 cups baby arugula

Directions

1. Combine the green goddess dressing ingredients in a blender and mix until smooth.

2. Combine marinade ingredients with the scallops in a bowl and toss to coat. Refrigerate 3 hrs.

3. Place the Grill Plate on the Power Smokeless Grill and preheat the Grill to 390° F.

4. Place the scallops on the Grill Plate and grill 2–4 mins. per side.

5. Divide the arugula between three plates and top evenly with scallops and green goddess dressing.

Eric's Tip: I like to add the leftovers the next day with some cooked pasta for a delicious salad.

Grilled Watermelon Salad

Ingredients

1 2 in.-thick slice watermelon with rind

1 cup microgreens

1 tbsp. extra virgin olive oil

1 tsp. lemon juice

sea salt and ground black pepper, to taste

1 cup feta cheese, crumbled

1 small red onion, thinly sliced

1 cup sliced strawberries

⅓ cup pine nuts, toasted

Directions

1. Place the Grill Plate on the Power Smokeless Grill and preheat the Grill to 350° F.

2. Place the watermelon on the Grill Plate and grill for 3–5 mins. per side.

3. Combine the microgreens, olive oil, lemon juice, salt, and ground black pepper in a bowl and toss together.

4. Sprinkle feta, red onion, strawberries, and pine nuts over the watermelon.

5. Top with microgreens and dressing.

6. Cut into slices before serving.

Eric's Tip: You can very easily turn this salad into an entrée by adding grilled chicken or shrimp, but my personal favorite is adding some thin sliced prosciutto.

Grilled Corn Salad

Ingredients

6 ears corn

½ red onion, diced

½ cup celery, diced

½ cup bell peppers, diced

2 tbsp. cilantro

1 clove fresh garlic, chopped

juice of ½ lime

¼ cup extra virgin olive oil

½ tsp. sea salt

½ tsp. ground black pepper

¼ cup sour cream, for garnish

Directions

1. Place the Grill Plate on the Power Smokeless Grill and preheat the Grill to 450° F.

2. Place the corn on the Grill Plate and cook until lightly charred (3–5 mins. per side).

3. Using a sharp knife, remove kernels from cobs.

4. Combine corn kernels, red onion, celery, red bell peppers, cilantro, garlic, lime juice, extra virgin olive oil, salt, and ground black pepper in a bowl, toss, and top with sour cream.

5. Serve with your favorite chicken, meat, and fish.

Eric's Tip: Another variation on this is to whiz it a few times with a hand blender or food processor, then substitute the sour cream for mayonnaise to make an interesting aioli. You can use it as a delicious sandwich spread or as a base for chicken salad.

Arugula Salad with Grilled Tomato Vinaigrette

Ingredients

12 slices bacon

2 pears, halved & cored

Tomato Vinaigrette

6 plum tomatoes, cut in half

½ cup extra virgin olive oil

1 tsp. sea salt

½ tsp. ground black pepper

3 cloves garlic, peeled & sliced

3 tbsp. red wine vinegar

———————

6 cups baby arugula

½ cup crumbled bleu cheese

⅓ cup pumpkin seeds, toasted

Directions

1. Place the Grill Plate on the Power Smokeless Grill and preheat the Grill to 390° F.

2. Place the bacon on the Grill Plate and cook until crispy. Remove.

3. Place the pears cut-side down on the Grill Plate and grill until lightly charred.

4. Combine tomatoes, extra virgin olive oil, salt, ground black pepper, and garlic in a bowl.

5. Place tomatoes on Grill and grill until charred, 3–5 mins. Remove, cool, then chop and add back into vinaigrette.

6. Stir red wine vinegar into the vinaigrette to finish.

7. Combine arugula, tomato vinaigrette, bleu cheese and pumpkin seeds. Toss gently.

8. Divide salad onto four plates and top each with 3 bacon slices and 1 pear half.

Eric's Tip: A grilled salmon or chicken breast turns this salad into the main course.

Grilled Bread Salad

Ingredients

Vinaigrette

½ cup extra virgin olive oil

¼ cup red wine vinegar

1 clove garlic, peeled & minced

salt & ground black pepper, to taste

---

1 French baguette, cut into 1 in.-thick slices

1 lb large cherry tomatoes, quartered

2 cucumbers, quartered & cut into 1-in. medallions

1 medium red onion, halved & sliced

¼ cup chopped fresh basil

Directions

1. Place the Grill Plate on the Power Smokeless Grill and preheat Grill to 350° F.

2. Combine the extra virgin olive oil, red wine vinegar, and garlic in a small bowl, and season to taste with salt and ground black pepper.

3. Place the baguette slices on the Grill Plate and cook each side until toasted. Remove and slice into quarters.

4. In a large bowl, toss together the cherry tomatoes, cucumbers, red onion, basil, baguette pieces, and vinaigrette. Serve immediately.

Eric's Tip: Drizzle some romaine hearts with salt, pepper and olive oil. Then grill for a few minutes to get a nice char.

Shrimp Po'Boy

Cheddar Jalapeño Stuffed
Burger

Buffalo Chicken Burger

Skirt Steak
& Tomato Tapenade Sandwich

Lamb & Goat Cheese Burger

Kimchi Korean Burger

Mac & Cheese Panini

Caramelized Mushroom Panini

Mozzarella & Pepperoncini
Stuffed Burger

Italian Panini

Philly Cheesesteak

Patty Melt

Chicken Broccoli Rabe Panini

SANDWICHES

Shrimp Po'Boy

Ingredients

Marinade

2 tbsp. olive oil

juice of 1 lemon

2 cloves garlic, peeled & minced

1 tsp. paprika

½ tsp. cumin

1 lb 21/25 shrimp

Remoulade

¼ cup mayonnaise

¼ cup Russian dressing

1 pinch seafood seasoning

1 pinch ground cayenne pepper

2 cups shredded lettuce

2 tomatoes, sliced

4 hoagie rolls, halved

Directions

1. Place the Griddle Plate on the Power Smokeless Grill and preheat the Grill to 390° F.

2. Combine the marinade ingredients in a bowl.

3. Coat the shrimp in the marinade, place the shrimp on the Griddle Plate, and cook shrimp for 3–5 mins. per side, until done.

4. Stir together the remoulade ingredients.

5. Assemble sandwiches: layer lettuce, tomato, shrimp, and remoulade sauce between rolls.

Griddle Recipe

Eric's Tip: The versatility of the Po'Boy Sandwich is endless. You can swap out the shrimp for any number of things. Grilled chicken, burgers, blackened catfish, pulled pork. . . they have it all in New Orleans!

Cheddar Jalapeño Stuffed Burger

Ingredients

Burger Mixture

2 lb ground beef

1 tsp. sea salt

1 tsp. ground black pepper

3 tbsp. chopped cilantro

½ small onion, peeled & minced

1 jalapeño, seeded & chopped

---

4 ½-oz cheddar cheese, cut into 4 chunks

2 tbsp. olive oil

4 slices cheddar cheese

4 brioche rolls, cut in half

¼ cup margarine

16 pickled jalapeño rings

Directions

1. Place the Grill Plate on the Power Smokeless Grill and preheat the Grill to 390° F.

2. Combine the burger mixture ingredients in a bowl and mix together. Form the burger mixture into four balls.

3. Stuff each ball with a chunk of cheddar cheese.

4. Rub burgers with olive oil, place the burgers on the Grill Plate, and grill each side to desired doneness (about 5 mins. per side).

5. Top each burger with 1 cheese slice during the last 2 mins. and top with the Glass Lid. Remove burgers.

6. Spread rolls with margarine, place the rolls (cut side down) on the Grill Plate, and grill until golden brown (2–3 mins.).

7. Assemble: top burgers with jalapeño rings and place between rolls.

Eric's Tip: If you have fresh sliced jalapeños, heat 1 cup vinegar and ¼ cup sugar, then pour over the peppers and let sit for 30 minutes for a quick pickle.

Buffalo Chicken Burger

Ingredients

Burger Mixture

2 lb ground chicken

2 tsp. kosher salt

1 tsp. ground black pepper

1 cup bleu cheese

3 tbsp. ranch dressing

2 tbsp. melted butter

¼ cup hot pepper sauce

1/2 cup panko

1 egg, beaten

———

2 tbsp. olive oil

¼ cup margarine

4 brioche rolls, cut in half

4 lettuce leaves

4 slices tomato

4 slices red onion

Directions

1. Place the Grill Plate on the Power Smokeless Grill and preheat the Grill to 350° F.

2. Combine the burger mixture ingredients in a bowl and mix together. Form mixture into four balls.

3. Rub burgers with olive oil, place on the Grill Plate, and grill to desired doneness (5–7 mins. per side). Remove.

4. Spread margarine on each brioche roll, place the rolls (cut side down) on the Grill Plate, and grill until golden brown (2–3 mins.).

5. Assemble: place burgers, lettuce, tomato, and red onion between each roll.

Eric's Tip: You can use any kind of ground meat with amazing results. Just adjust your cooking time accordingly.

Skirt Steak & Tomato Tapenade Sandwich

SERVES 3

Ingredients

Marinade

1 shallot, peeled & minced

3 tbsp. balsamic vinegar

¼ cup olive oil

½ tsp. sea salt

½ tsp. coarsely ground black pepper

_____

1 1-lb skirt steak

Tomato Red Onion Tapenade

¼ cup olive oil

2 tbsp. red wine vinegar

1 clove garlic, peeled & minced

½ tsp. sea salt

¼ tsp. ground black pepper

3 Roma tomatoes, chopped

¼ red onion, diced

6 basil leaves, chopped

_____

3 slices focaccia

Directions

1. Place the Grill Plate on the Power Smokeless Grill and preheat the Grill to 390° F.

2. Combine the marinade ingredients in a bowl.

3. Marinate the steak in the marinade for 1 hr. in the refrigerator.

4. Combine the tapenade ingredients in a bowl and reserve.

5. Place the steak on the Grill and grill to desired doneness. Let the steak rest for 10 mins. before slicing.

6. Place focaccia on the Grill and grill until toasted, 2 mins per side.

7. Assemble the sliced steak and tapenade on focaccia (open face).

Eric's Tip: Don't forget to let your steak rest for 5-10 minutes so it stays juicy. It's also important to slice the meat against the grain. For an extra special treat, add a little crumbled Gorgonzola cheese, I promise you won't be disappointed!

Lamb & Goat Cheese Burger

SERVES 3

Ingredients

Burger Mixture

1 lb ground lamb

½ onion, peeled & minced

2 sprigs rosemary, chopped

1 clove garlic, peeled & minced

2 tbsp. olive oil

1 tsp. sea salt

1 tsp. ground black pepper

4 oz goat cheese, crumbled

---

2 tbsp. margarine

3 brioche buns, cut in half

Directions

1. Place the Grill Plate on the Power Smokeless Grill and preheat the Grill to 390° F.

2. Combine the ground lamb, onion, rosemary, and garlic in a bowl. Form the mixture into three burgers.

3. Spread margarine on rolls, place (cut side down) on the Grill Plate, and grill until golden brown (2–3 mins.).

4. Brush each burger with olive oil and season with sea salt and ground black pepper.

5. Place the burgers on the Grill Plate and grill each side to desired doneness. Top with goat cheese.

6. Place a burger between each roll and serve with your favorite side dish.

Eric's Tip: If lamb is not available or just not to your liking, you can substitute any ground meat for this recipe. I've even ground up fresh fish in my food processor and made salmon sliders!

Kimchi Korean Burger

Ingredients

Burger Mixture

2 lb ground beef

2 tbsp. soy sauce

2 tbsp. brown sugar

½ cup chopped scallions

2 cloves garlic, peeled & minced

2 tbsp. sesame oil

2 tbsp. toasted sesame seeds

½ cup margarine

5 hamburger rolls

1 cup diced kimchi

Directions

1. Place the Grill Plate on the Power Smokeless Grill and preheat the Grill to 390° F.

2. Combine ground beef with soy sauce, brown sugar, scallions, garlic, sesame oil, and sesame seeds. Form into five patties.

3. Spread margarine onto the rolls, place (cut side down) on the Grill Plate, and grill until golden brown (2–3 mins.).

4. Place the burgers on the Grill Plate and grill to desired doneness.

5. Assemble each sandwich by placing the burgers and kimchi between each roll.

Eric's Tip: A lot of times you will see an egg garnish in traditional Korean cuisine. I can't think of anything better to top this burger than a nice farm-fresh egg served sunny side up!

Mac & Cheese Panini

Ingredients

2 cups heavy cream

½ tsp. sea salt

½ tsp. ground black pepper

2 tbsp. butter

1 tbsp. cornstarch

2 cups shredded cheddar cheese

2 cups macaroni elbows, cooked

½ cup margarine

8 slices white bread

16 slices yellow American cheese

Directions

1. Place the Grill Plate on the Power Smokeless Grill and preheat the Grill to 350° F.

2. Place a saucepan on the stove top over medium-high heat. Bring the cream, sea salt, ground black pepper, and butter to a boil.

3. Combine the cornstarch and cheddar cheese in a bowl and mix.

4. Add the cheese mixture to the boiling cream and whisk until creamy.

5. Add the cooked macaroni to the cheese sauce, turn off the heat, and stir.

6. Spread the margarine over one side of each bread slice.

7. Place 4 bread slices (buttered side down) on the Grill Plate and top each bread slice with 2 American cheese slices, about ¾ cup mac and cheese, 2 more American cheese slices, and 1 bread slice. Grill sandwiches on both sides until golden brown.

Eric's Tip: I love to mix in 1 cup of crispy crumbled bacon into the mac and cheese, then add a few tomato slices onto the sandwich.

Caramelized Mushroom Panini

Ingredients

1 lb button mushrooms, sliced

¼ cup extra virgin olive oil, divided

2 tsp. fresh thyme leaves

3 medium red onions, peeled & sliced

½ cup red wine

¼ cup beef broth

salt & ground black pepper, to taste

½ cup margarine

8 slices sourdough bread

16 slices Swiss cheese

Directions

1. Place the Grill Plate on the Power Smokeless Grill and preheat the Grill to 350° F.

2. In a frying pan on the stove top, sauté the mushrooms in 1 tbsp. olive oil until slightly tender.

3. Add the thyme and cook for 1 min. Remove and reserve the mushrooms in a bowl.

4. Add the remaining olive oil and the onions to the pan and sauté until tender (about 10 mins.)

5. Add the red wine and cook until fully absorbed.

6. Add beef broth and cook until fully absorbed.

7. Season with salt and ground black pepper.

8. Spread margarine on one side of each bread slice.

9. Place 4 bread slices (buttered side down) on the Grill Plate and top each with 2 Swiss cheese slices, onions, mushrooms, another 2 Swiss cheese slices, and 1 bread slice.

10. Grill on each side until golden brown.

Eric's Tip: The more variety the better. I love using a mix of mushrooms like shiitake, cremini and oyster mushrooms. Each has its own flavor and texture.

Mozzarella & Pepperoncini Stuffed Burger

Ingredients

Burger Mixture

2 lb ground beef

½ cup diced pepperoni

1 tsp. sea salt

1 tsp. ground black pepper

1 tsp. garlic powder

1 tsp. onion powder

2 tbsp. BBQ sauce

---

4 slices fresh mozzarella

2 tbsp. olive oil

¼ cup margarine

4 brioche rolls, cut in half

1 cup pepperoncini, for serving

Directions

1. Place the Grill Plate on the Power Smokeless Grill and preheat the Grill to 390° F.

2. Combine the burger mixture ingredients in a bowl. Form the burger mixture into four balls.

3. Stuff each ball with a slice of mozzarella.

4. Spread margarine inside each brioche roll, place the rolls (cut side down) on the Grill Plate, and grill until golden brown (2–3 mins.).

5. Rub the burgers with olive oil, place the balls on the Grill Plate, and grill each side to desired doneness.

6. Assemble by placing the burgers between rolls. Serve with the pepperoncini.

Eric's Tip: I love using a meatloaf mix of pork/beef/veal instead of the straight ground beef. It's available now at most markets.

Italian Panini

Ingredients

2 hoagie rolls, halved lengthwise

¼ cup margarine

½ cup baby spinach

8 thin slices tomato

¼ lb pepperoni, sliced

¼ lb salami, sliced

¼ lb ham, sliced

¼ lb provolone cheese, sliced

¼ cup hot cherry peppers

Olive Oil Dressing

¼ cup olive oil

2 tbsp. red wine vinegar

1 tsp. dried oregano

½ tsp. sea salt

½ tsp. ground black pepper

Directions

1. Place the Grill Plate on the Power Smokeless Grill and preheat the Grill to 350° F.

2. Butter the inside of each hoagie roll with the margarine, place the rolls (cut side down) on the Grill Plate, and grill until golden brown. Remove.

3. Top 2 hoagie roll halves with the spinach, tomatoes, pepperoni, salami, ham, provolone cheese, and cherry peppers.

4. Combine the olive oil dressing ingredients in a shaker bottle and shake.

5. Pour dressing evenly over the hoagie roll half and top with remaining roll halves.

6. Place the sandwiches on the Grill Plate and grill each side to desired doneness.

7. Serve with potato chips.

Eric's Tip: If you are really in the mood for something extra special, substitute the ham, pepperoni and salami for a quality mortadella.

Philly Cheesesteak

SERVES 2

Ingredients

1 large white onion, halved & sliced

1 tbsp. canola oil

½ lb ribeye steak, sliced very thinly

4 slices American cheese

2 hoagie rolls

kosher salt, to taste

ground black pepper, to taste

Directions

1. Place the Griddle Plate on the Power Smokeless Grill and preheat the Grill to 390° F.

2. Pour canola oil to the center of the Griddle Plate, add onions and sauté, tossing often, until onions begin to caramelize. Push the onions to one side of the Griddle Plate.

3. Place the steak on the Griddle Plate, season with salt and ground black pepper. and cook, tossing often, until cooked through (about 3 mins.) Push the steak to one side of the Griddle Plate.

4. Place 2 American cheese slices in the center of the Power Grill and top with half of the onion and half of the steak. Repeat with the rest of the cheese, onion, and steak.

5. Transfer the steak, onion, and cheese to the hoagie rolls.

Griddle Recipe

Patty Melt

Ingredients

2 6-oz hamburger patties

½ tsp. sea salt

½ tsp. ground black pepper

¼ cup margarine

4 slices rye bread

8 slices Swiss cheese

1 onion, sliced and sautéed

Directions

1. Place the Griddle Plate on the Power Smokeless Grill and preheat the Grill to 390° F.

2. Rub the burgers with the sea salt and ground black pepper.

3. Place the burgers on the Griddle Plate and grill each side to desired doneness. Remove.

4. Spread margarine onto one side of each bread slice

5. Assemble the sandwiches: arrange two slices of rye (margarine side down) on the Power Grill. Top each with two slices cheese, onions, a burger, two more slices cheese, and a second slice of rye.

6. Cook sandwiches until golden on each side.

7. Cut the sandwiches in half before serving.

Griddle Recipe

Chicken Broccoli Rabe Panini

Ingredients

2 cloves garlic, thinly sliced

3 tbsp. extra virgin olive oil

½ bunch broccoli rabe

½ tsp. sea salt

¼ tsp. red pepper flakes

8 slices fresh mozzarella

2 chicken breasts, cooked

2 ciabatta rolls, halved

Directions

1. Place the Griddle Plate on the Power Smokeless Grill and preheat the Grill to 390° F.

2. Add broccoli rabe and cook until tender.

3. Add the salt and red pepper flakes.

4. Assemble sandwiches: layer broccoli rabe, mozzarella, and chicken between each roll. Drizzle the inside of the paninis with the extra virgin olive oil from the sauté pan.

5. Place paninis on the Griddle Plate and cook on each side until golden brown.

6. Cut paninis in half before serving.

Griddle Recipe

QUESADILLAS

Teriyaki Chicken Quesadilla

Ingredients

Marinade

2 tbsp. teriyaki sauce

1 tbsp. orange juice concentrate

2 scallions, chopped

1 clove garlic, minced

½ tsp. red pepper flakes

1 tsp. ginger, minced

1 tsp. sesame oil

---

1 chicken breast, cut into
½ in. strips

2 8-in. tortillas

¾ cup shredded Monterey Jack
cheese

2 scallions, diced

3 tbsp. diced red pepper

1 tsp. chopped jalapeño

2 tbsp. salsa, for serving

2 tbsp. sour cream, for serving

¼ cup guacamole, for serving

Directions

1. Place the Griddle Plate on the Power Smokeless Grill and preheat the Grill to 390° F.

2. Combine the marinade ingredients in a bowl.

3. Marinate the chicken in the marinade for 1 hr. in the refrigerator.

4. Place the chicken on the Griddle Plate and grill until cooked through and registering 165° F. Allow chicken to rest, then dice.

5. Place 1 tortilla on the Griddle Plate and top with the Monterey Jack cheese, scallions, red pepper, and jalepeño. Top with the second tortilla. Grill quesadilla on each side until cheese is melted.

6. Cut into sections and serve with the salsa, sour cream, and guacamole.

Griddle Recipe

Eric's Tip: You can go vegetarian by replacing the chicken with firm tofu. Slice the tofu into 1 inch slices, then press between two plates lined with paper towels for 15 mins. After the excess moisture is drained, follow marinating and grilling instructions.

Mac & Cheese Quesadilla

Ingredients

2 cups heavy cream

2 cups shredded cheddar cheese

1 tbsp. cornstarch

2 tbsp. butter

2 cups elbow macaroni, cooked

4 8-in. tortillas

12 slices yellow American cheese

½ tsp. sea salt

½ tsp. ground black pepper

Directions

1. Place the Griddle Plate on the Power Smokeless Grill and preheat the Grill to 350° F.

2. Place a pot on the stovetop over medium-high heat. Bring the cream to a boil.

3. Combine the cheddar cheese and cornstarch in a bowl.

4. Add the butter and the cheese mixture to the hot cream and stir until creamy.

5. Add the macaroni and stir until well incorporated. Remove from the heat and let cool.

6. Place 2 tortillas on the Griddle Plate and top each tortilla with 3 slices American cheese, 1 cup mac and cheese, 3 more American cheese slices, the salt and ground black pepper, and another tortilla.

7. Grill quesadilla on both sides until the cheese is melted. Repeat with second tortilla.

Griddle Recipe

Eric's Tip: My absolute favorite variation on this recipe is to give a good sprinkle of seafood seasoning, plus some sweet corn and fresh crab meat for a Maryland-style quesadilla.

Turkey & Cranberry Quesadilla

SERVES 1

Ingredients

2 8-in. tortillas

¾ cup diced turkey breast

¼ cup cranberry sauce

½ cup shredded Monterey Jack cheese

1 tsp. chopped sage

2 tbsp. gravy, heated

½ cup mayonnaise

Directions

1. Place the Grill Plate on the Power Smokeless Grill and preheat the Grill to 350° F.

2. Place 1 tortilla on the Grill Plate and top with the turkey, cranberry sauce, Monterey Jack cheese, sage, and the other tortilla.

3. Grill quesadilla on both sides until the cheese is melted.

4. Combine the gravy and mayonnaise in a bowl.

5. Serve the quesadilla warm with the gravy.

Eric's Tip: Get some Texas toast and turn these quesadillas into a grilled cheese!

Greek Quesadilla

Ingredients

1 chicken breast, sliced in half

Greek Marinade

juice of ½ lemon

1 sprig oregano

½ tsp. salt

½ tsp. ground black pepper

2 tbsp. olive oil

2 8-in. tortillas

¼ cup crumbled feta cheese

½ cup shredded Monterey Jack cheese

2 pepperoncini peppers, sliced

½ cup cherry tomatoes, halved

2 tbsp. olives, halved

sour cream, for serving

Directions

1. Combine the marinade ingredients in a dish.

2. Marinate the chicken in the marinade for 20 mins. in the refrigerator.

3. Place the Grill Plate on the Power Smokeless Grill and preheat the Grill to 390 ° F.

4. Place the chicken on the Grill Plate and grill 3–4 mins. per side, until cooked through and registering 165 ° F. Remove, allow to cool, and then dice into small pieces.

5. Place 1 tortilla on the Grill Plate and top with the feta cheese, Monterey Jack cheese, pepperoncini, cherry tomatoes, olives, diced chicken, and the other tortilla. Grill quesadilla on each side until golden brown.

6. Cut the quesadilla and serve with sour cream.

Eric's Tip: Here is a dipping sauce that will make this even more flavorful. In a blender or food processor, combine 1 clove of garlic and ½ cup of plain yogurt with ½ cup of chopped cucumber, a ½ teaspoon of oregano, and the juice of half a lemon. Season to taste with salt and pepper.

Cheeseburger Quesadilla

Ingredients

1 lb ground beef

1 tbsp. Worcestershire sauce

1 tbsp. garlic powder

1 onion, peeled & diced

6 8-in. flour tortillas

18 slices American cheese

3 pickles, sliced

¼ cup ketchup

¼ cup mustard

Directions

1. Place the Griddle Plate on the Power Smokeless Grill and preheat the Grill to 350° F.

2. Sauté the ground beef, Worcestershire sauce, garlic powder, and onion for about 10 mins. Carefully remove meat.

3. Switch to the Grill Plate. Place 3 tortillas on the Grill Plate and top each tortilla with 3 American cheese slices, the cooked meat mixture, 1 pickle, the ketchup, mustard, and another tortilla.

4. Grill quesadillas on both sides until golden brown.

5. Serve warm with Eric's Dipping Sauce.

Griddle Recipe

Eric's Tip: My Not So Secret Dipping Sauce: combine 1 cup mayo, 3 tbsp. ketchup, 3 tbsp. relish, ¼ tsp. cayenne, 1 tsp. Dijon mustard, and ¼ tsp. garlic powder.

Vegetable Quesadilla

Ingredients

2 8-in. flour tortillas

2 tbsp. margarine

3 slices zucchini

3 mini peppers

4 Brussels sprouts

1 plum tomato, diced

¼ red onion

¼ jalapeño, diced

1 tbsp. chopped cilantro

¾ cup shredded cheddar jack cheese mix

2 tbsp. sour cream

½ tsp. lime zest

¼ tsp. sea salt

Directions

1. Place the Griddle Plate on the Power Smokeless Grill and preheat the Grill to 350° F.

2. Cook zucchini, mini peppers and Brussels sprouts until tender and lightly charred.

3. Spread each tortilla with the margarine.

4. Place 1 tortilla on the Griddle Plate and top with the zucchini, mini peppers, Brussels sprouts, tomato, red onion, jalapeño, cilantro, cheddar jack mix, and the other tortilla.

5. Cook quesadillas on each side until golden brown.

6. Combine the sour cream, lime zest, and salt in a small dish.

7. Cut the quesadilla and top with the sour cream before serving.

Griddle Recipe

Wild Mushroom Asiago Pizza

BBQ Chicken Pizza

Pesto White Pizza

Chicken Ranch Pizza

Mexican Pizza

Caramelized Onion, Pear
& Bleu Cheese Pizza

Spinach, Feta & Red Onion
Pizza

BLT Pizza

Margherita Pizza

Fig & Arugula Pizza

PIZZA

Wild Mushroom Asiago Pizza

Ingredients

3 portobello mushrooms

10 shiitake mushrooms

10 oyster mushrooms

1 thin-crust pizza dough

16 slices Asiago cheese

3 tbsp. grated Grana Padano cheese

4 cloves garlic, peeled & sliced very thinly

1 tsp. truffle salt

2 tbsp. extra virgin olive oil

Directions

1. Place the Griddle Plate on the Power Smokeless Grill and preheat the Grill to 320° F.

2. Place the shiitake and oyster mushrooms on the Griddle Plate and grill until tender. Remove the mushrooms, cool slightly, then chop and reserve.

3. Cut the pizza dough in half. Place half of the dough on the grill and cook until browned. Approximately 3 mins.

4. Flip the dough out onto a work surface and top with half of the mushrooms, cheeses, and sliced garlic. Return the pizza to the grill and cook for 2 mins. until the bottom of the dough is golden brown.

5. Turn the heat off, cover with the Glass Lid, and let sit until the cheese melts.

6. Once the cheese is melted, remove the pizza and serve. Repeat the process with the rest of the ingredients to make a second pizza.

Griddle Recipe

Eric's Tip: I absolutely love dried porcini mushrooms! Soaking 1 oz. of dried porcinis in ½ cup warm water will add that umami flavor to the pizza.

BBQ Chicken Pizza

Ingredients

2 small chicken breasts

½ cup BBQ sauce

1 red onion, peeled & sliced

2 tbsp. olive oil

1 thin-crust pizza dough

1 cup shredded cheddar cheese

4 scallions, chopped

Directions

1. Place the Griddle Plate on the Power Smokeless Grill and preheat the Grill to 320° F.

2. In a bowl, combine ¼ cup BBQ sauce with chicken. Grill until cooked through and registering 165° F. Allow to cool, then chop into pieces.

3. Toss the onions with olive oil. Grill to desired doneness.

4. Cut the pizza dough in half. Place half of the dough on the grill and cook until browned. Approximately 3 mins.

5. Flip the dough out onto a work surface and top with half of the chicken, onions, and cheese. Return the pizza to the grill and cook for 2 mins. until the bottom of the dough is golden brown.

6. Turn the heat off, cover with the Glass Lid, and let sit until the cheese melts.

7. Once the cheese is melted, remove the pizza and serve. Repeat the process with the rest of the ingredients to make a second pizza.

Griddle Recipe

Eric's Tip: Using a pre-made rotisserie chicken can save you some time if you don't want to cook the chicken breast.

Pesto White Pizza

Ingredients

1 thin-crust pizza dough

¼ cup pesto sauce

1 cup ricotta cheese

8 oz fresh mozzarella, thinly sliced

1 large Roma tomato, sliced thinly & cut into half-moons

2 tbsp. grated Parmesan cheese

1 pinch red pepper flakes

salt, to taste

ground black pepper, to taste

Directions

1. Place the Griddle Plate on the Power Smokeless Grill and preheat the Grill to 320° F.

2. Arrange dough on Griddle and grill for 3 mins.

3. Cut the pizza dough in half. Place half of the dough on the grill and cook until browned. Approximately 3 mins.

4. Flip the dough out onto a work surface and top with half of the pesto, ricotta, mozzarella, tomato, Parmesan, and pepper flakes. Return the pizza to the grill and cook for 2 mins. until the bottom of the dough is golden brown.

5. Turn the heat off, cover with the Glass Lid, and let sit until the cheese melts.

6. Once the cheese is melted, remove the pizza and serve. Repeat the process with the rest of the ingredients to make a second pizza.

Griddle Recipe

Eric's Tip: I love taking that leftover rotisserie chicken and adding it to this pizza.

Chicken Ranch Pizza

SERVES 6

Ingredients

1 thin-crust pizza dough

2 cups shredded cheddar cheese

2 cups cooked & shredded rotisserie chicken

4 strips bacon, cooked until crispy & crumbled

¼ cup sliced scallions

½ cup ranch dressing

Directions

1. Place the Grill Plate on the Power Smokeless Grill and preheat the Grill to 320° F.

2. Cut the pizza dough in half. Place half of the dough on the grill and cook until browned. Approximately 3 mins.

3. Flip the dough out onto a work surface and top with half of the cheese and chicken. Return the pizza to the grill and cook for 2 mins. until the bottom of the dough is golden brown.

4. Turn the heat off, cover with the Glass Lid, and let sit until the cheese melts.

5. Once the cheese is melted, remove the pizza and sprinkle with the bacon and scallions. Drizzle with the ranch dressing and serve. Repeat the process with the rest of the ingredients to make a second pizza.

Eric's Tip: Make it a club by topping with chopped lettuce, tomato and avocado!

Mexican Pizza

Ingredients

1 8-in. flour tortilla

½ cup salsa

1 cup shredded Mexican cheese blend

¼ cup black beans, drained & rinsed

1 link fully cooked chorizo, cut into thick medallions & quartered

¼ cup chopped scallions

2 tbsp. cilantro leaves

1 jalapeño, sliced

2 tbsp. Mexican crema

Directions

1. Place the Griddle Plate on the Power Smokeless Grill and preheat the Grill to 320° F.

2. Arrange tortilla onto Griddle and grill for for 2-3 mins.

3. Flip tortilla and spread with salsa. Top with cheese, beans, and chorizo.

4. Cover with the Glass Lid and continue cooking for 4 mins. until the cheese melts.

5. Top with scallions, cilantro, and sliced jalapeño. Drizzle with crema immediately before serving.

Griddle Recipe

Eric's Tip: For a lighter version you can substitute chorizo with turkey or chicken sausage.

Caramelized Onion, Pear & Bleu Cheese Pizza

Ingredients

2 red onions, peeled & sliced

3 tbsp. butter

1 thin-crust pizza dough

2 pears, cored & sliced

1 cup bleu cheese

2 cups arugula

2 tbsp. extra virgin olive oil

½ tsp. sea salt

½ tsp. ground black pepper

Directions

1. In a sauté pan, caramelize red onions in butter.

2. Place the Grill Plate on the Power Smokeless Grill and preheat the Grill to 320° F.

3. Cut the pizza dough in half. Place half of the dough on the grill and cook until browned. Approximately 3 mins.

4. Flip the dough out onto a work surface and top with half of the onions, pears, and cheese. Return the pizza to the grill and cook for 2 mins. until the bottom of the dough is golden brown.

5. Turn the heat off, cover with the Glass Lid, and let sit until the cheese melts.

6. Once the cheese is melted, remove the pizza. Top with arugula and drizzle with extra virgin olive oil before serving. Repeat the process with the rest of the ingredients to make a second pizza.

Eric's Tip: Don't let the bleu cheese scare you away, it's amazing in this dish. There are many varieties, so talk to your local cheesemonger to find one that suits your taste.

Spinach, Feta & Red Onion Pizza

SERVES 6

Ingredients

1 thin-crust pizza dough

5 oz baby spinach

¼ cup extra virgin olive oil

1 clove garlic, peeled & minced

½ cup crumbled feta cheese

1 small red onion, halved & thinly sliced into half moons

¼ cup Kalamata olives, halved

¼ cup chopped sun-dried tomatoes

salt & ground black pepper, to taste

Directions

1. Place the Grill Plate on the Power Smokeless Grill and preheat the Grill to 320° F.

2. In a sauté pan, sauté spinach lightly with olive oil and garlic.

3. Cut the pizza dough in half. Place half of the dough on the grill and cook until browned. Approximately 3 mins.

4. Flip the dough out onto a work surface and top with half of the spinach, feta, onion, olives, and sundried tomatoes. Return the pizza to the grill and cook for 2 mins. until the bottom of the dough is golden brown.

5. Turn the heat off, cover with the Glass Lid, and let sit until the cheese melts.

6. Once the cheese is melted, remove the pizza and serve. Repeat the process with the rest of the ingredients to make a second pizza.

Eric's Tip: I love adding baby arugula to this pizza. Layer it under the feta before cooking, or use it as a garnish after cooking.

BLT Pizza

Ingredients

1 thin-crust pizza dough

9 slices provolone cheese

½ lb bacon

1 red onion, peeled, sliced

12 tomato slices

2 cups shredded lettuce

2 tbsp. mayonnaise

Directions

1. Place the Grill Plate on the Power Smokeless Grill and preheat the Grill to 320° F.

2. Place bacon on the Grill and grill until crisp. Reserve grease.

3. Place onion onto the Grill and grill until tender. Reserve.

4. Cut the pizza dough in half. Place half of the dough on the grill and cook until browned. Approximately 3 mins.

5. Flip the dough out onto a work surface and top with half of the cheese and bacon grease. Return the pizza to the grill and cook for 2 mins. until the bottom of the dough is golden brown.

6. Turn the heat off, cover with the Glass Lid, and let sit until the cheese melts.

7. Once the cheese is melted, remove the pizza and and layer pizza with bacon, tomato, onion, and lettuce. Drizzle with mayonnaise before serving. Repeat the process with the rest of the ingredients to make a second pizza.

Eric's Tip: Don't forget the diced ripe avocado! And feel free to make it lighter by using grilled chicken or turkey bacon.

Margherita Pizza

Ingredients

1 thin-crust pizza dough

2 tbsp. basil pesto

2 vine-ripe tomatoes, sliced

14 slices fresh mozzarella

1 clove garlic, peeled & sliced thinly

1 tbsp. olive oil

Directions

1. Place the Griddle Plate on the Power Smokeless Grill and preheat the Grill to 320° F.

2. Cut the pizza dough in half. Place half of the dough on the grill and cook until browned. Approximately 3 mins.

3. Flip the dough out onto a work surface and top with half of the pesto, tomatoes, mozzarella, garlic, and oil. Return the pizza to the grill and cook for 2 mins. until the bottom of the dough is golden brown.

4. Turn the heat off, cover with the Glass Lid, and let sit until the cheese melts.

5. Once the cheese is melted, remove the pizza and serve. Repeat the process with the rest of the ingredients to make a second pizza.

Griddle Recipe

Fig & Arugula Pizza

Ingredients

1 thin-crust pizza dough

3 tbsp. fig spread

½ cup crumbled bleu cheese

1 cup arugula

2 tbsp. extra virgin olive oil

Directions

1. Place the Griddle Plate on the Power Smokeless Grill and preheat the Grill to 320° F.

2. Cut the pizza dough in half. Place half of the dough on the grill and cook until browned. Approximately 3 mins.

3. Flip the dough out onto a work surface and top with half of the fig spread and cheese. Return the pizza to the grill and cook for 2 mins. until the bottom of the dough is golden brown.

4. Turn the heat off, cover with the Glass Lid, and let sit until the cheese melts.

5. Once the cheese is melted, remove the pizza and top with arugula and olive oil before serving. Repeat the process with the rest of the ingredients to make a second pizza.

Griddle Recipe

Sticky Sesame
Ginger Chicken Wings

Chili Lime Spatchcock Chicken

Tomato & Pesto Stuffed
Chicken Breast

Tomato & Olive Grilled Thighs

Spicy BBQ Brick Chicken

Tandoori Chicken Skewers

Sweet & Spicy Smoked
Chicken Thighs

Pesto Chicken Paillard

Italian Chicken & Panzanella

Blackened Chicken Breast
with Mango Salsa

CHICKEN

Sticky Sesame Ginger Chicken Wings

SERVES 4

Ingredients

Sesame Ginger Sauce

1 cup sweet chili sauce

1 tbsp. fresh ginger, grated

1 tbsp. sesame oil

½ tbsp. chili paste

2 tbsp. honey

1 tbsp. lime juice

2 lbs chicken wings, split

1 tbsp. sesame seeds

2 scallions, sliced

Directions

1. Place the Grill Plate on the Power Smokeless Grill and preheat the Grill to 390° F.

2. To make the sauce, in a bowl, combine sweet chili sauce, ginger, sesame oil, chili paste, honey, and lime juice.

3. Grill wings until fully cooked through and crispy, and registering 165° F. Toss with sesame ginger sauce.

4. Sprinkle with sesame seeds and scallions before serving.

Eric's Tip: This marinade also works well with chicken breasts and thighs if you want to add it to a salad, sandwich or tacos.

Chili Lime Spatchcock Chicken

SERVES 2

Ingredients

Chili Lime Rub

2 tbsp. chili powder

1 tsp. coriander

1 tsp. cumin

1 tsp. paprika

2 tsp. garlic powder

1 tsp. onion powder

3 tbsp. lime juice

2 tsp. lime zest

¼ cup olive oil

½ tbsp. sea salt

1 tsp. ground black pepper

1 3-lb chicken, backbone removed and flattened

Directions

1. Place the Grill Plate on the Power Smokeless Grill and preheat the Grill to 350° F.

2. Chili lime spice: in a bowl, combine all spice ingredients.

3. Rub chicken all over with spice mixture.

4. Place chicken on Grill skin-side down. Cover and cook the chicken 15 mins. per side, or until chicken registers 165° F internally.

5. Allow chicken to rest for 15 mins. before serving.

Eric's Tip: You always want to let cooked meat rest before slicing so the juices redistribute back into the meat. If you cut it too soon, all the juice will run out which will result in a dry chicken.

Tomato & Pesto Stuffed Chicken Breast

SERVES 4

Ingredients

Pesto

1 cup basil

3 tbsp. cup parsley

2 tbsp. pine nuts, toasted

2 cloves garlic

¼ cup grated Parmesan cheese

½ cup extra virgin olive oil

1 tsp. sea salt

¼ tsp. ground black pepper

---

4 small boneless & skinless chicken breasts

1 tbsp. extra virgin olive oil

2 Roma tomatoes, sliced into rounds

8 oz fresh mozzarella, sliced into rounds

1 cup baby spinach

salt & ground black pepper, to taste

Directions

1. In a food processor, combine all pesto ingredients and blend.

2. Place the Grill Plate on the Power Smokeless Grill and preheat the Grill to 350° F.

3. Slice into each chicken breast lengthwise to make a pocket for the stuffing.

4. Rub the inside of each breast with pesto. Layer with tomato, mozzarella cheese, and spinach.

5. Season the outside of the chicken with salt and pepper, to taste and drizzle with olive oil.

6. Grill the chicken breasts for 4-5 mins. per side until chicken reaches an internal temperature of 165° F.

7. Allow chicken to rest for 5 mins. before serving.

Eric's Tip: Serve this chicken in between some fresh baked focaccia for the best Italian grinder.

Tomato & Olive Grilled Thighs

SERVES 4

Ingredients

Marinade

½ onion, peeled & minced

2 cloves garlic, peeled & minced

2 sprigs rosemary

3 sprigs thyme

¼ cup apple cider vinegar

½ cup olive oil

2 tbsp. soy sauce

3 tbsp. honey

1 tsp. ground black pepper

8 chicken thighs, boneless
& skinless

Tomato and Olive Salad

3 tomatoes, diced

½ cup chopped Kalamata olives

1 clove garlic, peeled & minced

¼ red onion, peeled & minced

½ head fennel, diced small

6 basil leaves, chopped

1 tsp. sea salt

½ tsp. ground black pepper

Directions

1. Combine all marinade ingredients in a bowl. Marinate chicken in the refrigerator for 6 hrs.

2. Place the Grill Plate on the Power Smokeless Grill and preheat the Grill to 350° F.

3. Grill chicken for about 7 mins. on both sides, or until internal temperature reaches 165° F.

4. Combine tomato and olive salad ingredients in a bowl, and serve with chicken.

Eric's Tip: I love to pair this dish with grilled romaine hearts or radicchio.

Spicy BBQ Brick Chicken

SERVES 2

Ingredients

Spicy BBQ Sauce

1 cup BBQ sauce

2 tbsp. Sriracha sauce

½ tsp. liquid smoke

1 tsp. garlic powder

1 tsp. onion powder

1 tsp. salt

1 tsp. ground black pepper

1 3-lb chicken, backbone removed and flattened

Directions

1. Place the Grill Plate on the Power Smokeless Grill and preheat the Grill to 350° F.

2. In a bowl, mix together all BBQ sauce ingredients. Pour over the chicken, turning to coat.

3. Arrange the chicken skin-side down onto the Power Grill.

4. Top with a heavy brick or weight wrapped in foil, or a cast iron pan.

5. Cook for about 15 mins. skin-side down, then flip chicken and cover with the Glass Lid. Cook 15 more mins. or until internal temperature reaches 165° F. Allow to rest at least 15 mins.

Eric's Tip: When I make brick chicken, I'll make sure to rub some of the marinade between the meat and skin.

Tandoori Chicken Skewers

SERVES 8

Ingredients

Tandoori Marinade

1 cup plain yogurt

1 ½ tsp. garam masala

¼ tsp. cayenne pepper

2 tbsp. grated yellow onion

1 tsp. grated garlic

1 tsp. grated ginger

juice of ½ lemon

2 lb chicken breast, cubed

2 scallions, sliced for garnish

Directions

1. Tandoori marinade: in a bowl, combine yogurt, garam masala, cayenne, onion, garlic, ginger, and lemon juice.

2. Marinate chicken in the marinade overnight in the refrigerator.

3. Place the Grill Plate on the Power Smokeless Grill and preheat the Grill to 390 ° F.

4. Thread chicken onto skewers.

5. Grill chicken skewers on all sides until cooked to 165° F internal temperature.

6. Let the skewers rest, then garnish with scallions. Serve with a salad or traditional side dishes.

Eric's Tip: For the best chicken salad, chill in the refrigerator after grilling. Hand shred the chicken, then mix with chopped onion, celery, dried cranberries, and a touch of mayonnaise.

Sweet & Spicy Smoked Chicken Thighs

SERVES 4

Ingredients

Sweet & Spicy Sauce

⅓ cup molasses

1 tbsp. cider vinegar

2 tbsp. melted butter

2 cloves garlic, peeled & minced

½ onion, peeled & minced

1 tsp. red pepper flakes

1 tsp. hot pepper sauce

½ tsp. liquid smoke

2 lb chicken thighs

Directions

1. Place the Grill Plate on the Power Smokeless Grill and preheat the Grill to 390 ° F.

2. Combine sauce ingredients in a bowl.

3. Coat chicken thighs with sauce, reserving a little for basting, and arrange on Grill.

4. Grill on both sides until chicken reaches 165° F internal temperature. Baste with a few spoonfuls of additional sauce and grill five more mins.

5. Serve chicken thighs with your favorite vegetable.

Eric's Tip: If you want to give these thighs an autumnal feel, replace molasses with 5 cups fresh apple cider cooked down to ⅓ cup.

Pesto Chicken Paillard

Ingredients

Marinade

¼ cup olive oil

2 tbsp. red wine vinegar

½ tsp. ground black pepper

1 tsp. sea salt

4 tbsp. pesto

---

2 small chicken breasts, halved lengthwise & pounded ¼ in. thick

4 tbsp. pesto

Salad

3 tbsp. extra virgin olive oil

juice of ½ lemon

½ tsp. ground black pepper

½ tsp. sea salt

1 cup arugula

2 cups mesclun mix

¼ cup shaved Parmigiano-Reggiano cheese

½ cup cherry tomatoes, halved

Directions

1. Place the Grill Plate on the Power Smokeless Grill and preheat the Grill to 390° F.

2. Combine chicken with marinade and refrigerate for 1-2 hrs.

3. Grill chicken on each side until cooked through. Chicken will cook quickly as it is very thin.

4. Remove chicken from the Grill Plate. Brush with pesto and allow to rest.

5. Combine salad ingredients in a large bowl.

6. Serve chicken over the salad.

Eric's Tip: I love tossing the salad with fresh cooked pasta to gently wilt the greens to make it an entrée.

Italian Chicken & Panzanella

SERVES 2–4

Ingredients

Marinade

1 tbsp. Italian seasoning

1 tsp. sea salt

1 tsp. ground black pepper

1 tsp. garlic powder

1 tsp. onion powder

2 tbsp. olive oil

2 small chicken breasts, trimmed

Panzanella Salad

½ baguette, sliced lengthwise

1 pint grape tomatoes

1 seedless cucumber, cubed

2 tbsp. parsley, chopped

4 large basil leaves, chiffonade

¼ cup red wine vinegar

½ cup extra virgin olive oil

1 tsp. salt

1 tsp. ground black pepper

1 clove garlic, peeled & minced

1 red onion, peeled & sliced thinly

Directions

1. Place the Grill Plate on the Power Smokeless Grill and preheat the Grill to 390° F.

2. In a bowl, combine marinade ingredients. Coat the chicken on both sides with the marinade.

3. Grill chicken for 5-7 mins. per side until cooked through and registering 165° F. Allow chicken to rest.

4. Grill the baguette until crispy. Cut into cubes.

5. Slice the chicken. Toss with remaining salad ingredients and bread cubes before serving.

Eric's Tip: Panzanella salad was originally created by the resourceful Italian Grandmothers to use up day-old bread.

Blackened Chicken Breast with Mango Salsa

Ingredients

Mango Salsa

1 mango, peeled & diced small

¼ red onion, diced

¼ red pepper, diced

1 tbsp. chopped cilantro

¼ jalapeño, minced

2 tbsp. mango juice

6 small chicken breasts

3–4 tbsp. blackened seasoning

Directions

1. Place the Griddle Plate on the Power Smokeless Grill and preheat the Grill to 390° F.

2. Combine mango salsa ingredients in a bowl. Set aside.

3. Season the chicken generously with blackened spice.

4. Grill chicken on both sides until cooked through, 165° F.

5. Allow chicken to rest, then slice and serve with mango salsa.

Griddle Recipe

Grilled Salmon
with Cider & Shallots

Shrimp Tacos
& Cilantro Aioli

Grilled Salmon
& Chorizo Vinaigrette

Shrimp & Sausage Skewers

Sweet & Spicy
Bacon-Wrapped Catfish

Mustard-Marinated Swordfish
with Spinach

Tilapia & Corn Salsa

Grilled Tuna & Lime
Cilantro Butter Sauce

Curry Coconut Scallops

Grilled Mahi Mahi
with Eric's Fish Rub

Sweet Sriracha Shrimp Tacos

Garlic Lime Shrimp

Salmon with Mustard-Dill
Compound Butter

FISH & SEAFOOD

Grilled Salmon with Cider & Shallots

Ingredients

Cider Marinade

1 shallot, peeled & minced

1 tbsp. soy sauce

2 tbsp. apple cider

1 tsp. crushed peppercorns

juice of 1 lemon

6 5-oz salmon fillets

Cider & Shallot Sauce

2 tbsp. butter

4 shallots, peeled & sliced

1 cup cider

¼ cup white wine

1 sprig tarragon, chopped

1 tbsp. chopped parsley

1 bay leaf

½ tsp. kosher salt

¼ tsp. ground black pepper

Directions

1. Place the Grill Plate on the Power Smokeless Grill and preheat the Grill to 390° F.

2. In a bowl, combine salmon with marinade ingredients. Marinate in the refrigerator for 1 hr.

3. Remove salmon from marinade. Pat dry with a paper towel.

4. Grill for about 6 mins. per side, until just opaque, or to desired doneness.

5. Make the sauce: in a frying pan, sauté shallots in butter until translucent.

6. Add remaining sauce ingredients. Reduce by two-thirds.

7. Spoon sauce over the salmon. Serve with your favorite side dish.

Eric's Tip: Making sure the fish is completely dry from the marinade is key to beautiful grill marks. For that professional restaurant-looking cross-hatch, turn the salmon a quarter turn after the initial 3 mins. of grilling on the first side.

Shrimp Tacos & Cilantro Aioli

Ingredients

1 lb 21–25 shrimp, peeled & deveined

1 tbsp. seafood seasoning

1 tsp. onion powder

½ tsp. sea salt

½ tsp. ground black pepper

2 tbsp. extra virgin olive oil

Cilantro Aioli

¼ cup mayonnaise

1 tsp. hot sauce

1 tbsp. cilantro, chopped

1 clove fresh garlic chopped

4 6-in. flour tortillas

fresh cilantro, for serving

fresh lime, for serving

Taco Toppings

1 cup chopped cabbage

1 yellow pepper, seeded & diced

¼ red onion, peeled & minced

1 plum tomato, diced

Directions

1. Place the Grill Plate on the Power Smokeless Grill and preheat the Grill to 350° F.

2. Toss the shrimp with seafood seasoning, onion powder, sea salt, pepper, and olive oil.

3. Grill shrimp on both sides, until cooked through.

4. In a bowl, stir together aioli ingredients. Set aside.

5. Assemble the tacos: spread some aioli onto each tortilla.

6. Layer with cabbage, yellow pepper, onion, tomato, and shrimp.

7. Serve with limes and fresh cilantro leaves.

Eric's Tip: Depending on my mood and what's fresh at the market, I'll substitute the shrimp for scallops or lobster. Don't forget the crumbled queso fresco!

Grilled Salmon & Chorizo Vinaigrette

SERVES 4

Ingredients

Chorizo Vinaigrette

½ cup extra virgin olive oil, divided

2 links chorizo, diced

2 tsp. minced garlic

1 pinch ground coriander

¼ cup scallions

1 tbsp. chopped cilantro

juice of 1 lime

salt, to taste

ground black pepper, to taste

---

4 6-oz salmon fillets, skin on

salt, to taste

ground black pepper, to taste

Directions

1. Place the Griddle Plate on the Power Smokeless Grill and preheat the Grill to 390° F.

2. Heat 1 tbsp. olive oil and fry the chorizo on the Griddle 5 mins. until crisp. Add garlic, coriander, and scallions to the griddle. Add cilantro and lime juice then remove from the heat.

3. Switch to the Grill Plate. Season the salmon filets with salt and pepper and place on the Grill skin side down.

4. Cover with the Glass Lid and cook 4-5 mins. per side.

5. Serve with Chorizo Vinaigrette.

Eric's Tip: Serve this over a delicious mushroom risotto or mixed greens salad. It works both hot and cold!

Shrimp & Sausage Skewers

SERVES 4

Ingredients

24 16–20 shrimp, peeled
& deveined

juice of 1 lime

1 clove garlic, peeled & minced

½ tsp. sea salt

½ tsp. ground black pepper

6 sprigs cilantro, minced

2 chorizo sausage links, sliced

Directions

1. Place the Grill Plate on the Power Smokeless Grill and preheat the Grill to 390° F.

2. Combine shrimp with lime juice, garlic, sea salt, pepper, and cilantro. Marinate in the refrigerator for 1 hr.

3. Assemble skewers by alternating pieces of shrimp and sausage.

4. Grill skewers about 4-5 mins. per side.

5. Serve with rice or your favorite side dish.

Eric's Tip: Using smoked or cured sausage will prevent the shrimp from overcooking. If you can only get raw sausage, pre-cook and cool then slice into chunks.

Sweet & Spicy Bacon-Wrapped Catfish

SERVES 2

Ingredients

2 cups spinach

2 5-oz fillets catfish

4 slices bacon

Sweet & Spicy Glaze

2 tbsp. sweet chili sauce

1 tbsp. sweet soy sauce

1 tbsp. rice vinegar

1 tsp. chipotle powder

½ onion, peeled & minced

Directions

1. Place the Griddle Plate on the Power Smokeless Grill and preheat the Grill to 390° F.

2. Place spinach, a pinch of salt, and 1 tbsp. water onto Griddle and cover with lid. Let steam, then cool.

3. Lay each catfish fillet flat. Spoon half of the spinach on top of each. Roll fillet around spinach to make a roulade.

4. Wrap two slices bacon around each roulade.

5. Place roulades on Grill, and grill about 5-8 mins. per side.

6. Combine glaze ingredients in a bowl. Spoon generously over fish.

7. Serve with any remaining glaze and your favorite side dish.

Eric's Tip: Call me crazy, but when I was developing this recipe, I put the catfish in a nice fresh long roll to make an awesome Po' Boy. Just add some shredded lettuce and sliced tomato!

Mustard-Marinated Swordfish with Spinach

SERVES 8

Ingredients

Mustard Marinade

2 shallots, peeled & minced

1 tbsp. mustard seeds

¼ cup white wine vinegar

2 sprigs tarragon

¾ cup olive oil

½ tbsp. honey

1 tsp. sea salt

½ tsp. crushed black peppercorns

8 6-oz swordfish steaks

10 cups spinach

½ cup cherry tomatoes, halved, for garnish

Directions

1. Make marinade: bring shallot, mustard seeds, vinegar, and tarragon to a boil in a saucepan. Remove and set aside to cool completely. Once cool, stir in olive oil, honey, sea salt, and peppercorns. Mix well.

2. Pour half of the marinade over the swordfish steaks. Reserve remaining marinade for serving.

3. Allow fish to marinate in the refrigerator for 3 hrs.

4. Place the Griddle Plate on the Power Smokeless Grill and preheat the Grill to 390° F.

5. Add the spinach, 1 tbsp. water and a pinch of salt to the Griddle, cover with the lid and allow to steam. Remove from heat.

6. Switch to the Grill Plate. Grill swordfish steaks on each side until just cooked through, about 3-4 mins per side, depending on thickness.

7. Plate swordfish over spinach and top with remaining marinade. Sprinkle with cherry tomatoes before serving.

Eric's Tip: You can use any quality IQF (individually quick frozen) fish in this recipe such as mahi mahi, tuna, or salmon. Thaw and adjust grilling time according to directions.

Tilapia & Corn Salsa

Ingredients

Corn Salsa

3 ears corn

4 scallions, chopped

6 sprigs cilantro, chopped

juice of 1 lime

1 tsp. sea salt

½ red pepper, seeded & chopped

½ jalapeño, chopped

---

4 4-oz tilapia fillets

Eric's Fish Rub

½ tsp. sea salt

½ tsp. onion powder

½ tsp. thyme

½ tsp. tarragon

½ tbsp. dried parsley

½ tbsp. dried cilantro

½ tsp. ground white pepper

1 tsp. dried lemon peel

½ tsp. celery seeds

Directions

1. Place the Grill Plate on the Power Smokeless Grill and preheat the Grill to 390° F.

2. Grill corn on all sides until lightly charred. Cool, then remove kernels from the cobs. Combine corn with rest of salsa ingredients in a bowl. Toss and set aside.

3. Rub tilapia gently with the fish rub. Grill 2-4 mins. per side, or until opaque and just cooked through.

4. Serve fish with corn salsa.

Eric's Tip: I love experimenting with the fish rub. I'll add some cayenne or dried habanero for an extra kick. For a Mediterranean feel, I'll throw in some ground fennel and anise seed.

Grilled Tuna & Lime Cilantro Butter Sauce

SERVES 4

Ingredients

Marinade

1 tbsp. coriander, seeds

1 tbsp. ground black pepper

1 tbsp. garlic powder

3 tbsp. grapeseed oil

2 tbsp. soy sauce

1 lime, juiced

———

4 8-oz tuna steaks, center cut

Cilantro Lime Butter Sauce

1 stick butter

1 shallot, peeled & chopped

juice of 1 lime

½ tsp coriander powder

½ tsp. Sriracha sauce

½ tsp. sea salt

½ tsp. chipotle powder

3 tbsp. chopped cilantro

Directions

1. In a bowl, combine tuna with marinade. Marinate in the refrigerator for 30 mins.

2. Place the Grill Plate on the Power Smokeless Grill and preheat the Grill to 390° F.

3. Remove tuna from marinade. Pat dry with paper towels.

4. Place tuna on Grill and grill for about 3–5 mins. per side.

5. Allow tuna to rest, then slice.

6. In a saucepan, sauté shallot with 2 tbsp. butter. Add lime juice, coriander, Sriracha, sea salt, and chipotle powder. Cook until reduced by half, then turn off the heat. Whisk in remaining butter and chopped cilantro.

7. Spoon sauce generously over tuna to serve.

Eric's Tip: In most recipes, substitutions can be made. In this, I really stand firm in using a high-quality tuna steak. Cooking the tuna to a nice medium rare is my favorite preference. Most markets now carry sushi-grade tuna so don't skimp and treat yourself!

Curry Coconut Scallops

Ingredients

Coconut Curry Sauce

1 tbsp. olive oil

2 cloves garlic, peeled & minced

2 tbsp. red curry

1 can coconut milk

2 scallions, chopped

juice of ½ lime

1 tbsp. fish sauce

2 ½ lb scallops

1 tbsp. cumin

1 tbsp. sea salt

1 tbsp. ground black pepper
scallions, chopped, for garnish

Directions

1. **Sauce:** in a saucepan, sauté the garlic in olive oil for 2 mins. until slightly golden.

2. Add remaining sauce ingredients and cook until slightly thickened. Set sauce aside.

3. Place the Grill Plate on the Power Smokeless Grill and preheat the Grill to 390° F.

4. Season scallops with cumin, sea salt, and pepper.

5. Place scallops on Grill and grill about 2 mins. per side, or to desired doneness.

6. Serve scallops with coconut curry sauce. Garnish with scallions.

Eric's Tip: I love to serve these scallops over Thai rice noodles garnished with fresh bean sprouts and cilantro.

Grilled Mahi Mahi with Eric's Fish Rub

SERVES 4

Ingredients

Eric's Fish Rub

1 tbsp. crushed sea salt

1 tbsp. onion powder

1 tsp. thyme

2 tsp. tarragon

1 tbsp. dried parsley

1 tbsp. dried chives

1 tbsp. ground white pepper

1 tbsp. dried lemon peel

1 tsp. celery seeds

---

4 5-oz fillets mahi mahi

Directions

1. Place the Grill Plate on the Power Smokeless Grill and preheat the Grill to 390° F.

2. In a bowl, combine the spices. Rub evenly over both sides of the mahi mahi.

3. Grill mahi mahi to desired doneness, about 3–5 mins. per side.

4. Serve fish with Grilled Peach & Pineapple Salsa.

Eric's Tip: Serve with warm flour tortillas and cabbage slaw for fantastic tacos.

Sweet Sriracha Shrimp Tacos

Ingredients

1 lb 21–25 shrimp, peeled & deveined

1 tsp. Sriracha powder

1 tsp. onion powder

½ tsp. ground coriander

4 6-in. flour tortillas

Sriracha Sauce

1 tsp. Sriracha sauce

¼ cup mayonnaise

1 tsp. honey

1 tsp. lime juice

1 tbsp. chopped cilantro

Toppings

1 cup red cabbage, chopped

1 avocado, sliced

½ cup diced mango

4 scallions, chopped

¼ red onion, peeled & chopped

lime wedges, to serve

cilantro leaves, to serve

Directions

1. Place the Grill Plate on the Power Smokeless Grill and preheat the Grill to 390 ° F.

2. Toss the shrimp with Sriracha powder, onion powder, and coriander.

3. Place shrimp on the Grill and grill to desired doneness, 2-3 mins. per side.

4. In a bowl, combine sauce ingredients and set aside.

5. Assemble the tacos: spread Sriracha sauce onto each tortilla, and layer with cabbage, avocado, mango, scallion, red onion, and shrimp.

6. Serve tacos with limes and fresh cilantro leaves.

Eric's Tip: Substitute the shrimp for cubed salmon or swordfish for a different flavor profile.

Garlic Lime Shrimp

SERVES 6

Ingredients

Marinade

zest & juice of 2 limes

¼ cup olive oil

2 tbsp. chopped cilantro

2 cloves garlic, minced

¼ tsp. red pepper flakes

_____

2 lb 16–20 shrimp, peeled
& deveined

Directions

1. Combine shrimp with marinade in a re-sealable plastic bag. Refrigerate for 2 hrs.

2. Place the Griddle Plate on the Power Smokeless Grill and preheat the Grill to 390° F.

3. Remove shrimp from the marinade and pat dry with paper towels.

4. Place shrimp on the Griddle Plate and grill for about 2-3 mins. per side, or to desired doneness.

5. Serve shrimp with rice. Use leftovers for tacos.

Griddle Recipe

Salmon with Mustard-Dill Compound Butter

Ingredients

Marinade

¼ cup olive oil

2 tbsp. soy sauce

juice of 1 lemon

1 shallot, peeled & minced

_____

6 6-oz salmon fillets

Compound Butter

1 stick salted butter

1 tbsp. Dijon mustard

½ tsp. ground black pepper

1 shallot, peeled & minced

1 tbsp. chopped fresh dill

Directions

1. In a re-sealable plastic bag, combine fish with marinade. Place in the refrigerator 1-3 hrs.

2. In a bowl, mix compound butter ingredients together. Set aside.

3. Place the Griddle Plate on the Power Smokeless Grill and preheat the Grill to 390° F.

4. Remove salmon from marinade. Pat dry with paper towels.

5. Place salmon on Griddle Plate and grill about 4-5 mins. per side, to desired doneness.

6. Top each fillet with a tbsp. of compound butter before serving.

Griddle Recipe

24-Hour Marinated
Flat Iron Steaks

Herb-Grilled London Broil

Pork Chops
with Dried Plums & Shallots

Grilled Cowboy Steak
with Eric's Herb Salt Rub

Cherry Tomato Pork
Tenderloin

Chimichurri Sirloin Steak

Mediterranean Pork Chops

Lamb Loin Chops
with Eric's Red Meat Rub

Eric's Surf & Turf

Grilled Skirt Steak
with Salsa Verde

Hanger Steak
& Green Peppercorn Butter

Flank Steak
with Balsamic Onion Dressing

Grilled Filet
with Porcini Compound Butter

Filet with Mushrooms
& Shallots

MEATS

24-Hour Marinated Flat Iron Steaks

Ingredients

Marinade

1 clove garlic, peeled & chopped

1 shallot, peeled & chopped

1 tsp. ground black pepper

1 tsp. sea salt

3 tbsp. balsamic vinegar

¼ cup extra virgin olive oil

2 sprigs rosemary

2 lb flat iron steak

Eric's Herb Salt Rub

1 cup course sea salt

2 tbsp. black peppercorns

3 sprigs rosemary

4 sprigs thyme

1 sprig sage

2 sprigs tarragon

1 clove garlic, peeled

Directions

1. In a re-sealable plastic bag, combine steak with all marinade ingredients. Refrigerate overnight.

2. Place the Grill Plate on the Power Smokeless Grill and preheat the Grill to to 390° F.

3. Grill steak to desired temperature. Let rest 10 mins. before slicing.

4. Remove herbs from stems. Blend salt rub ingredients together in a food processor. Any remaining rub can be kept in a sealed container and used for meat or fish.

5. Drizzle with extra virgin olive oil and sprinkle with some of Eric's Herb Salt before serving.

Eric's Tip: Flat Iron steaks cook quickly so be careful not to overcook. About 5-7 minutes per side should get you to a nice medium rare. I love this steak chilled the next day in a sandwich or salad.

Herb-Grilled London Broil

Ingredients

Marinade

2 sprigs rosemary, leaves chopped

4 sprigs thyme, leaves chopped

¼ cup pesto

1 tbsp. kosher salt

1 tbsp. course ground black pepper

2 tsp. extra virgin olive oil

3 lb London broil

Directions

1. Combine marinade ingredients.

2. In a re-sealable plastic bag, rub steak with marinade, being sure to coat all sides. Refrigerate for 2 hrs. or up to 24 hrs.

3. Place the Grill Plate on the Power Smokeless Grill and preheat Grill to 390° F.

4. Place London broil on the Grill and grill about 9 mins. per side or to desired temperature.

5. Let rest for 10 mins. before slicing thinly across the grain.

6. Serve with your favorite side dish or in a delicious sandwich.

Eric's Tip: If you want an extra special treat, make yourself a London broil club sandwich!

Pork Chops with Dried Plums & Shallots

SERVES 6

Ingredients

Plum Sauce

1 cup dried plums

1 cup red wine

1 tbsp. butter

2 shallots, peeled & sliced

3 sprigs thyme

½ cup port wine

½ cup chicken broth

⅓ cup rice wine vinegar

¼ cup cream

6 center cut pork chops

1 tbsp. sea salt

½ tbsp. ground black pepper

Directions

1. In a small bowl, combine dried plums with red wine. Soak for 30 mins.

2. In a saucepan, sauté shallots in butter for 2 mins. or until tender.

3. Add plums, thyme, port wine, chicken broth, and rice wine vinegar to shallots. Cook until reduced by half. Add the cream. Reduce again until slightly thickened. Set sauce aside.

4. Place the Grill Plate on the Power Smokeless Grill and preheat the Grill to 390° F.

5. Season pork chops with salt and pepper.

6. Place pork chops on Grill and grill until temperature reaches 145° F. Allow to rest.

7. Drizzle pork chops with plum sauce.

8. Serve with grilled carrots or your favorite vegetable.

Eric's Tip: With the availability of dried fruits, the variations are almost endless. If you don't like dried plums, use dried figs. If you don't like figs, use dried apricots.

Grilled Cowboy Steak with Eric's Herb Salt Rub

SERVES 2

Ingredients

Eric's Herb Salt Rub

1 cup course ground sea salt

2 tbsp. black peppercorns

3 sprigs rosemary

4 sprigs thyme

1 sprig sage

2 sprigs tarragon

1 clove garlic, peeled

2 lb. cowboy steak (bone-in, ribeye, trimmed)

Directions

1. Remove herbs from stems. Blend salt rub ingredients together in a food processor.

2. Place the Grill Plate on the Power Smokeless Grill and preheat the Grill to 390° F,

3. Rub the steak with ½ tbsp. salt rub on each side. Any remaining rub can be kept in a sealed container and used for meat or fish.

4. Grill steak on each side for 7 mins. or until desired doneness.

5. Let steak rest for 10 mins. before slicing and serving.

Eric's Tip: While the steak is resting on a separate plate, degrease the pan and then deglaze with 1 cup of white wine and reduce. Remove the pan from the heat and swirl in 2 tablespoons of butter for some awesome sauce!

Cherry Tomato Pork Tenderloin

SERVES 2

Ingredients

Marinade

1 clove garlic, peeled & minced

3 tbsp. olive oil

2 sprigs rosemary, chopped

1 tbsp. cider vinegar

1 tsp. sea salt

1 tsp. ground black pepper

2 1 ½ lb pork tenderloins

Sauce

1 tbsp. olive oil

1 clove garlic, peeled & minced

1 pint cherry tomatoes, halved

1 sprig tarragon, chopped

½ cup Kalamata olives, halved

½ cup chicken broth

¼ cup white wine

1 tbsp. white balsamic vinegar

1 tbsp. honey

1 tsp. Dijon mustard

2 tbsp. butter

Directions

1. Place the Grill Plate on the Power Smokeless Grill and preheat the Grill to 390° F.

2. Combine marinade ingredients. Marinate pork in the refrigerator for 1 hr.

3. Place the pork on the Grill and grill until internal temperature reaches 145° F-155° F approximately 30–40 mins. Allow to rest.

4. Sauce: in a saucepot, sauté the garlic in olive oil until lightly golden.

5. Add tomatoes and toss for 2 mins. Add remaining sauce ingredients and reduce by half.

6. Spoon sauce over pork tenderloin before serving.

Eric's Tip: Allow pork tenderloin to rest for 15 mins. before slicing.

Chimichurri Sirloin Steak

SERVES 2

Ingredients

Chimichurri Sauce

½ cup fresh Italian parsley

¼ cup olive oil

2 tbsp. red wine vinegar

¼ cup fresh cilantro

1 garlic clove, peeled

½ tsp. dried crushed red pepper

½ tsp. ground cumin

½ tsp. salt

---

2 12-oz NY strip steaks

1 tsp. sea salt

1 tsp. course ground black pepper

Directions

1. Place the Grill Plate on the Power Smokeless Grill and preheat the Grill to 390° F.

2. Combine chimichurri sauce ingredients in a blender and blend until well incorporated.

3. Season steaks with salt and pepper. Grill about 7 mins. on each side, or to desired doneness.

4. Let steaks rest for 10 mins. before slicing.

5. Top steak with chimichurri sauce just before serving.

Eric's Tip: If you aren't a fan of cilantro, you can substitute any herb such as basil or thyme. You can make a Chimichurri Rojo by adding tomato or red pepper purée.

Mediterranean Pork Chops

Ingredients

6 thick-cut pork chops

¼ cup olive oil

1 tbsp. sea salt

1 tsp. ground black pepper

Salad

½ cup Kalamata olives

1 clove garlic, peeled & minced

1 pint cherry tomatoes, quartered

1/4 cup feta cheese

3 tbsp. red wine vinegar

1 sprig fresh oregano

¼ cup extra virgin olive oil

1 cup cannellini beans

Directions

1. Place the Grill Plate on the Power Smokeless Grill and preheat the Grill to 390° F.

2. Rub pork chops with olive oil, sea salt, and pepper.

3. Place chops on the Grill and grill about 5-7 mins. per side or until internal temperature reaches 145° F-155° F.

4. In a bowl, combine all salad ingredients. Toss.

5. Serve pork chops with salad and your favorite side dishes.

Eric's Tip: I love spooning the salad over couscous or tabbouleh for a complete meal.

Lamb Loin Chops with Eric's Red Meat Rub

SERVES 4

Ingredients

Eric's Red Meat Rub

2 tbsp. crushed sea salt

2 tbsp. brown sugar

2 tbsp. ground black coffee

1 tbsp. granulated garlic

1 tbsp. granulated onion

1 tbsp. cumin

1 tbsp. coriander

1 tbsp. ground black pepper

12 lamb loin chops

Directions

1. Place the Grill plate on the Power Smokeless Grill and preheat the Grill to 390° F.

2. Distribute rub evenly over the lamb chops.

3. Place the lamb on the Grill, cover with the lid and grill 5-7 mins. per side, or to desired temperature.

4. Let rest 10 mins. before serving with your favorite side dishes.

Eric's Tip: Try using this with a nice thick tuna steak!

Eric's
Surf & Turf

Ingredients

Eric's Red Meat Rub

¼ cup sea salt

¼ cup brown sugar

¼ cup ground black coffee

2 tbsp. granulated garlic

3 tbsp. granulated onion

1 tbsp. cumin, ground

1 tbsp. coriander

1 tbsp. ground black pepper

Eric's Fish Rub

½ tsp. sea salt

½ tsp. onion powder

½ tsp. thyme

½ tsp. tarragon

½ tbsp. dried parsley

½ tbsp. dried chives

½ tsp. ground white pepper

½ tsp. dried lemon peel

½ tsp. celery seeds

2 10-oz rib eye steaks

2 6-oz lobster tails

lemon wedges, for serving

Directions

1. Place the Grill plate on the Power Smokeless Grill and preheat the Grill to to 390° F.

2. Cover steaks with red meat rub on each side.

3. Sprinkle lobster with fish rub.

4. Place steaks and lobster on Grill and grill until desired temperature.

5. Serve with lemon wedges and your favorite side dishes.

Eric's Tip: The whole thing about surf and turf is that you can use any cut of meat, fish or seafood. You can tailor it to your personal tastes and to what is fresh or available at the market.

Grilled Skirt Steak with Salsa Verde

Ingredients

Marinade

juice of 2 limes

4 cloves garlic, peeled & chopped

1 tbsp. ground coriander

10 sprigs cilantro, chopped

½ cup olive oil

1 tbsp. sea salt

1 tbsp. Sriracha sauce

2 1-lb skirt steaks

Salsa Verde

8 tomatillos, husked & rinsed

2 serrano peppers

½ small onion, peeled & chopped

1 clove garlic, peeled

8 sprigs fresh cilantro

1 tsp. sea salt

juice of ½ lime

Directions

1. Combine all marinade ingredients together and add steaks. Marinate in the refrigerator for 1-2 hrs.

2. Place the Grill Plate on the Power Smokeless Grill and preheat the Grill to 390° F.

3. Grill the tomatillos, peppers, garlic, and onions until tender and charred. Puree in a blender with remaining salsa ingredients. Set aside.

4. Remove steak from marinade. Pat dry with paper towels. Grill 5-7 mins. per side or to desired doneness.

5. Let rest 10 mins. before slicing. Serve steak warm with salsa verde.

Eric's Tip: For the best street tacos, add warmed corn tortillas, chopped red onion and crumbled queso fresco.

Hanger Steak & Green Peppercorn Butter

SERVES 4

Ingredients

2 lb hanger steak

1 tbsp. sea salt

1 tbsp. coarse ground black peppercorns

¼ cup olive oil

Bleu Cheese Green Peppercorn Butter

½ lb butter

¼ cup crumbled bleu cheese

1 tbsp. chopped green peppercorns

1 shallot, peeled & minced

½ tbsp. Dijon mustard

Directions

1. Place the Grill Plate on the Power Smokeless Grill and preheat the Grill to 390° F.

2. Rub the steak with sea salt, pepper, and olive oil.

3. In an electric mixer, blend butter ingredients until creamy.

4. Place steaks on the Grill and grill to desired temperature.

5. Allow steaks to rest before slicing. Top with peppercorn butter immediately before serving.

Eric's Tip: Don't forget to slice the meat against the grain or you will risk a tough piece of steak.

Flank Steak with Balsamic Onion Dressing

SERVES 6

Ingredients

Balsamic Onion Dressing

6 cipollini onions, peeled

¼ cup balsamic vinegar

½ cup extra virgin olive oil

1 sprig thyme, chopped

1 tsp. sea salt

½ tsp. ground black pepper

1 tsp. sugar

---

1 flank steak

1–2 tsp. sea salt

1 tsp. ground black pepper

2 tbsp. olive oil

Directions

1. Place the Grill Plate on the Power Smokeless Grill and preheat the Grill to 390° F.

2. Rub Flank steak with sea salt, pepper, and olive oil.

3. Mix balsamic onion dressing ingredients together.

4. Using a slotted spoon, remove onions from dressing and grill until tender (about 10 mins.). Cool slightly, then cut onions into quarters before returning to the dressing.

5. Place steaks on the Grill and grill to desired temperature.

6. Let steaks rest before slicing. Drizzle with dressing before serving with your favorite side dish.

Eric's Tip: If you can't find cipollini onions, you can substitute frozen pearl onions. Just make sure they're thawed and patted dry.

Grilled Filet with Porcini Compound Butter

SERVES 8

Ingredients

Compound Butter

¼ cup dried porcini mushrooms

½ cup red wine

½ shallot, peeled & diced

½ tsp. sea salt

½ tsp. ground black pepper

2 sprigs tarragon, chopped

½ lb sweet butter, softened

½ tbsp. Dijon mustard

---

8 6-oz beef tenderloin filets

1 tbsp. sea salt

½ tbsp. ground black pepper

Directions

1. Place the Grill Plate on the Power Smokeless Grill and preheat the Grill to 390° F.

2. In a saucepot, combine mushrooms, red wine, and shallot. Bring to a boil and reduce by ²/₃. Set aside to cool.

3. Combine sea salt, black pepper, tarragon, butter, and Dijon mustard in a bowl. Stir in mushroom mixture and set aside.

4. Season filets with sea salt and pepper.

5. Place steaks on the Grill and grill for 4-5 mins. per side or to desired temperature.

6. Top filets with butter before serving.

7. Roll leftover compound butter in wax paper and store in the freezer for future use.

Eric's Tip: Mix this butter into rice, pasta, veggies or even make an awesome garlic bread with it. My favorite is to mash it into a baked potato.

Filet with Mushrooms & Shallots

SERVES 6

Ingredients

6 beef filets, 6 oz.

2 tbsp. olive oil

1 tbsp. sea salt

1 tbsp. ground black pepper

1 lb. cremini mushrooms

2 shallots, peeled & minced

2 tbsp. butter, soft

2 sprigs rosemary

Directions

1. Place the Griddle Plate on the Power Smokeless Grill and preheat the Grill to 390° F for 4 mins.

2. Rub the filets with olive oil, sea salt, and pepper.

3. Sear the filets on each side, about 5-7 minutes or to desired temperature. Plate filets and set aside.

4. Cook mushrooms and shallots on the Griddle Plate with butter and rosemary, 6-7 minutes.

5. Serve filets with mushrooms and shallots.

Griddle Recipe

Shishito Peppers
with Feta & Herbs

Lemony Asparagus
with Basil & Oregano

Grilled Corn with Cilantro Aioli

Grilled Eggplant Parm

Grilled Veggie Kabobs

Chipotle-Grilled
Cauliflower Steaks

Grilled Asparagus & Feta

Zucchini Fritters

VEGGIES

Shishito Peppers with Feta & Herbs

SERVES 4

Ingredients

½ lb shishito peppers

½ cup extra virgin olive oil

4 cloves garlic, peeled & sliced

1 tsp. sea salt

½ tsp. hot red pepper flakes

½ cup crumbled feta cheese

1 sprig rosemary, chopped

2 sprigs thyme, chopped

Directions

1. Place the Grill Plate on the Power Smokeless Grill and preheat the Grill to 350° F.

2. In a bowl, combine peppers with olive oil, garlic, sea salt, and red pepper flakes.

3. Using a slotted spoon, place peppers and garlic on the Grill and grill until charred and tender. Reserve remaining olive oil in the bowl.

4. Plate garlic and peppers. Sprinkle with remaining olive oil, feta, and herbs.

5. Serve peppers alone or with your favorite protein (I recommend the Skirt Steak).

Eric's Tip: Don't be afraid of the shishito pepper. It's only a little hotter than a bell pepper, well below a jalapeño.

Lemony Asparagus with Basil & Oregano

SERVES 4

Ingredients

1 lb asparagus

3 tbsp. extra virgin olive oil

1 tsp. sea salt

½ tsp. red pepper flakes

½ tsp. granulated garlic powder

½ tsp. dried oregano

6 basil leaves, chopped

zest of ½ lemon

juice of ½ lemon

Directions

1. Place the Grill Plate on the Power Smokeless Grill and preheat the Grill to 350° F.

2. Toss asparagus with olive oil, sea salt, red pepper flakes, and garlic powder.

3. Place asparagus on Grill and grill until tender and lightly charred.

4. Sprinkle asparagus with oregano, basil, lemon zest, and lemon juice immediately before serving.

Eric's Tip: If fresh asparagus isn't available, you can substitute fresh green beans or even baby bok choy.

Grilled Corn with Cilantro Aioli

Ingredients

4 ears corn, shucked

Cilantro Aioli

1 cup mayonnaise

½ cup packed fresh cilantro

1 clove garlic, peeled

1 cup feta cheese

1 tbsp. Sriracha, for serving

Directions

1. Place the Grill Plate on the Power Smokeless Grill and preheat the Grill to 450° F.

2. Place corn on the Grill and cover with the glass lid. Grill corn on all sides.

3. Cilantro aioli: in a blender, combine mayonnaise, cilantro, and garlic until smooth.

4. Brush the corn with aioli and roll in feta cheese.

5. Drizzle with Sriracha before serving.

Eric's Tip: After grilling, slice into 2-inch sections then skewer the cobb for "lollipop" style appetizers.

176

Grilled Eggplant Parm

Ingredients

1 large eggplant (8 slices)

1 cloves garlic, peeled & minced

¼ cup olive oil

2 tbsp. red wine vinegar

1 tsp. kosher salt

¼ tsp. ground black pepper

8 tomato slices

8 mozzarella slices

2 tbsp. grated Parmigiano-Reggiano cheese

1 cup marinara sauce, heated

8 basil leaves

Directions

1. In a bowl, marinate the eggplant with garlic, olive oil, vinegar, sea salt, and pepper for 1 hr.

2. Place the Grill Plate on the Power Smokeless Grill and preheat the Grill to 350° F.

3. Drain the marinade from the eggplant.

4. Arrange eggplant onto the Grill Plate. Grill on both sides until charred and cooked through.

5. Layer eggplant with tomato, mozzarella, and Parmigiano. Cover with the Glass Lid, reduce the heat to 320° F, and cook until the cheese melts.

6. Serve warm with marinara sauce.

Eric's Tip: I love adding grilled zucchini, yellow squash and portobello mushrooms for a Primavera Parmigiana.

Grilled Veggie Kabobs

SERVES 6

Ingredients

1 red pepper, diced large

1 yellow pepper, diced large

1 zucchini, cut into 1-in. rounds

1 yellow squash, cut into 1-in. rounds

12 medium mushrooms

1 red onion, diced large

Marinade

¾ cup cider vinegar

2 tbsp. basil, chopped

2 tbsp. parsley, chopped

2 cloves garlic, peeled & minced

1 tbsp. sea salt

1 tsp. ground black pepper

Directions

1. Skewer the vegetables.

2. Marinade: in a bowl, combine vinegar, herbs, garlic, sea salt, and pepper. Pour over vegetable skewers. Marinate for 1 hr. at room temperature.

3. Place the Grill Plate on the Power Smokeless Grill and preheat the Grill to 350 ° F.

4. Drain the marinade from the kabobs. Arrange kabobs on the Power Grill, and grill, rotating until vegetables are tender.

Eric's Tip: I always have a warm pita schmeared with hummus ready to wrap around the kabobs when they come hot off the Grill Pan.

Chipotle-Grilled Cauliflower Steaks

SERVES 4

Ingredients

1 large head cauliflower,
sliced into 1 in.-thick steaks

Marinade

½ cup extra virgin olive oil

2 tbsp. rice wine vinegar

2 tbsp. lime juice, divided

2 cloves garlic, peeled & minced

Chipotle Rub

2 tbsp. kosher salt

1 tsp. ground black pepper

1 tsp. chipotle powder

¼ cup cilantro leaves, chopped,
to serve

Directions

1. Place the Grill Plate on the Power Smokeless Grill and preheat the Grill to 350° F.

2. In a pan, marinate the cauliflower with olive oil, vinegar, 1 tbsp. lime juice, and garlic for 1 hr. at room temperature.

3. Chipotle rub: in a separate bowl, combine sea salt, pepper, and chipotle powder.

4. Drain the marinade from the cauliflower. Sprinkle with chipotle rub.

5. Place cauliflower on the Grill and grill about 7 mins. per side until crisp and tender.

6. Sprinkle cauliflower with cilantro before serving.

Eric's Tip: I'll swap the chipotle for curry powder to give this dish an exotic, Middle Eastern flair.

Grilled Asparagus & Feta

Ingredients

1 lb asparagus, trimmed

¼ cup extra virgin olive oil

½ tsp. sea salt

½ tsp. ground black pepper

juice of 1 lemon

½ cup crumbled feta cheese

¼ cup pine nuts, lightly toasted

1 tsp. dried oregano

Directions

1. Place the Grill Plate on the Power Smokeless Grill and preheat the Grill to 350° F.

2. Coat asparagus with olive oil. Season with salt and pepper.

3. Place asparagus on the Grill until and grill until tender and charred.

4. Sprinkle asparagus with lemon juice, feta, pine nuts, and dried oregano before serving.

Eric's Tip: If fresh asparagus is not available, green beans can be substituted.

Zucchini Fritters

Ingredients

1 zucchini, shredded

⅓ cup flour

⅓ cup grated Parmesan cheese

2 eggs

¼ tsp. sea salt

½ tsp. ground black pepper

½ small onion, diced

1 clove garlic, peeled & minced

3 tbsp. olive oil

Directions

1. Place the Griddle Plate on the Power Smokeless Grill and preheat the Grill to 350° F.

2. In a bowl, combine all ingredients except olive oil.

3. Coat the Griddle Plate with olive oil.

4. Drop heaping tablespoons of fritter batter onto the Griddle.

5. Cook on both sides until golden.

Griddle Recipe

Banana Split Pizza

Grilled Cinnamon S'mores
Toast

Salted Caramel
Peanut Butter Sundae

Grilled Doughnut Triple Decker
Ice Cream Sandwich

Grilled Banana Split Sundae

Grilled Peaches & Berries
Over Vanilla Ice Cream

Apple Pie Panini

Grilled Pound Cake & Fruit

Grilled Fruit Skewers

Grilled Strawberry Shortcake

Grilled Pineapple Sundae

Brioche French Toast

Grilled Apple Bowls
& Vanilla Ice Cream

Sweet Potato Pancakes

French Toast Sundae

DESSERTS

Banana
Split Pizza

SERVES 8

Ingredients

8 oz thin-crust pizza dough

¼ cup caramel sauce

2 bananas, sliced

8 strawberries, halved

2 tbsp. chocolate sauce

2 tbsp. raspberry sauce

¼ cup chopped peanuts

Directions

1. Place the Grill Plate on the Power Smokeless Grill and preheat the Grill to 320° F.

2. Place strawberries and bananas on Grill and grill until lightly charred. Remove to cool.

3. Place pizza dough onto the the Grill. Cook 3 minutes, flip, and cook an additional 3-5 minutes. Remove.

4. Spread caramel sauce over the pizza. Layer with bananas and strawberries.

5. Drizzle with chocolate and raspberry sauces. Top with peanuts.

6. Cut pizza into 8 slices. Serve alone or with your favorite ice cream.

Eric's Tip: Sprinkling toasted coconut or crumbled graham crackers will add extra flavor and crunch!

Grilled Cinnamon S'mores Toast

SERVES 2

Ingredients

½ cup sugar

1 tbsp. cinnamon

4 slices white bread

¼ cup margarine

15 baby marshmallows

1 4-oz chocolate bar

Directions

1. Place the Grill Plate on the Power Smokeless Grill and preheat the Grill to 350° F.

2. Combine sugar and cinnamon in a bowl.

3. Spread margarine over one side of each slice of bread. Sprinkle with cinnamon and sugar mixture.

4. Arrange two slices of bread onto the Grill, margarine side down. Cover each slice with marshmallows and half of the chocolate bar.

5. Top with remaining two slices of bread. Grill 3 mins. per side, until chocolate and marshmallows are melted.

6. Serve alone or with a tall glass of milk.

Eric's Tip: As if this couldn't get any better, try a little peanut butter inside!

Salted Caramel Peanut Butter Sundae

MAKES 4

Ingredients

4 bananas, peeled & sliced into medallions

4 large scoops vanilla ice cream

½ cup creamy peanut butter

½ cup caramel sauce

¼ cup chopped peanuts

pink sea salt, to sprinkle

Directions

1. Place the Grill Plate on the Power Smokeless Grill and preheat the Grill to 390° F.

2. Place bananas on the Grill and grill until caramelized.

3. Scoop ice cream into a serving bowl. Top with bananas, peanut butter, caramel sauce, and chopped peanuts.

4. Sprinkle lightly with pink sea salt before serving.

Eric's Tip: Sprinkle the bananas with cinnamon and cayenne pepper before grilling for a little kick!

Grilled Doughnut Triple Decker Ice Cream Sandwich

SERVES 4

Ingredients

4 apple cider doughnuts, sliced in half

2 pears, halved, cored & sliced

4 cups vanilla ice cream, slightly softened

½ cup chocolate sauce

whipped cream, for serving

Directions

1. Place the Grill Plate on the Power Smokeless Grill and preheat the Grill to 350° F.

2. Arrange doughnut and pears halves on the Grill and grill to desired doneness.

3. Place the ice cream into a small baking pan and cover with plastic wrap. Press to about 2 inches thick, then freeze.

4. Cut frozen ice cream into 8 discs the same size as the doughnuts.

5. Place one doughnut half onto each dish. Layer with sliced pears and ice cream. Top with a second doughnut half. Repeat to make it a triple decker.

6. Drizzle with chocolate sauce and whipped cream before serving.

Eric's Tip: The key to this recipe is to use the best seasonal fruit. Local orchards and farm stands will keep the variety of this recipe endless!

Grilled Banana Split Sundae

SERVES 2

Ingredients

Strawberry Sauce

8 oz strawberries

2 tsp. sugar

Pineapple Sauce

8 oz pineapple rounds

¼ cup light brown sugar

Sundae Basics

4 bananas, halved lengthwise

vanilla ice cream

chocolate ice cream

chocolate sauce

½ cup chopped peanuts

whipped cream

Directions

1. Place the Grill Plate on the Power Smokeless Grill and preheat the Grill to 350° F.

2. Place strawberries, pineapple, and banana halves onto the Grill and grill to desired doneness. Set aside.

3. Strawberry sauce: in a small saucepan, combine the grilled strawberries with sugar. Cook until sugar is dissolved and strawberries are blended.

4. Pineapple sauce: in a separate saucepan, combine the grilled pineapples with light brown sugar. Cook until sugar is dissolved and pineapples are blended.

5. Assemble the sundae: line a dish with grilled bananas.

6. Top with 3 scoops vanilla and / or chocolate ice cream and fruit sauces.

7. Sprinkle with peanuts. Top with chocolate sauce and whipped cream before serving.

Eric's Tip: I love using this grilled fruit sauce to flavor my margaritas!

Grilled Peaches & Berries Over Vanilla Ice Cream

SERVES 2

Ingredients

Simple Syrup

½ cup water

½ cup sugar

1 cinnamon stick

1 tbsp. orange liqueur

2 peaches, halved & pitted

6 strawberries, halved

vanilla ice cream

––––––––

½ cup fresh blueberries, for garnish

mint, for garnish

Directions

1. Simple syrup: bring water, sugar, and cinnamon stick to a boil. Add orange liqueur. Remove from heat.

2. Combine peaches and strawberries in a bowl with simple syrup. Soak for 1 hr. at room temperature.

3. Place the Grill Plate on the Power Smokeless Grill and preheat the Grill to 350° F.

4. Place strawberries and peaches on the Grill and grill until tender.

5. Top ice cream with grilled fruit. Garnish with blueberries and fresh mint immediately before serving.

Eric's Tip: I love combining flatbread, chocolate hazelnut spread, and grilled fruit for an amazing dessert pizza!

Apple Pie Panini

SERVES 4

Ingredients

8 slices white bread

4 tbsp. butter, softened

2 Granny Smith apples, cored, halved & sliced thinly

¼ cup brown sugar

1 tsp. cinnamon

½ cup cream cheese, softened

2 cups vanilla ice cream

Directions

1. Place the Grill Plate on the Power Smokeless Grill and preheat the Grill to 350° F.

2. Brush the bread on one side with butter.

3. In a bowl, combine the apples, brown sugar, and cinnamon. Mix.

4. Spread cream cheese thinly on the un-buttered side of the bread.

5. Assemble the paninis with the apple mixture and second slice of bread.

6. Place paninis on the Grill and grill each side until golden.

7. Cut paninis in half before serving with vanilla ice cream.

Eric's Tip: I love trying different cheeses with this recipe. Yellow cheddar and Brie are my two favorites!

Grilled Pound Cake & Fruit

SERVES 6

Ingredients

6 slices pound cake

3 peaches, sliced & pitted

3 bananas, peeled & sliced

24 large strawberries

½ cup simple syrup

¼ cup raspberry sauce

1 cup whipped cream

6 mint leaves, for garnish

Directions

1. Place the Grill Plate on the Power Smokeless Grill and preheat the Grill to 350° F.

2. Arrange the pound cake, peaches, bananas, and strawberries on the Grill. Cook on both sides to desired doneness.

3. Toss the fruit with simple syrup. Set aside.

4. Plate the pound cake with the grilled fruit.

5. Top with raspberry sauce and whipped cream. Garnish with mint leaves immediately before serving.

Eric's Tip: Another delicious variation on this recipe is to slice a corn muffin in half and grill. The fruit and cream complement the corn's sweetness.

Grilled Fruit Skewers

Ingredients

8 large strawberries

2 peaches, thickly sliced

1 pear, thickly sliced

1 cup pineapple, cubed

1 banana, thickly sliced

Chocolate Dipping Sauce

1 cup heavy cream

1 cup semisweet chocolate chips

½ tsp. vanilla extract

Directions

1. Place the Grill Plate on the Power Smokeless Grill and preheat the Grill to 350° F.

2. Skewer the cut fruit. Place skewers on the Grill and grill to desired doneness.

3. Dipping sauce: in a saucepot, bring the heavy cream to a boil. Add the chocolate chips and remove from heat.

4. Stir until creamy, then add vanilla.

5. Serve grilled fruit with chocolate dipping sauce.

Eric's Tip: Feel free to choose any chocolate you like. Dark and white work well with this recipe.

Grilled Strawberry Shortcake

Ingredients

1 angel food cake, sliced into wedges

½ stick butter

1 lb strawberries, cut in half

zest of 1 lemon

juice of ½ lemon

1 tbsp. sugar

1 ½ cup heavy cream

¼ cup confectioners' sugar, to whip cream

1 tsp. vanilla extract

Directions

1. Place the Grill Plate on the Power Smokeless Grill and preheat the Grill to 350° F.

2. Brush the cake wedges with butter and place on the Grill. Grill to desired doneness.

3. Grill the strawberries. Allow to cool, then toss with lemon zest, lemon juice, and 1 tbsp. sugar.

4. Whip the cream with ¼ cup confectioners' sugar and vanilla.

5. Top cake wedges with strawberries and whipped cream immediately before serving.

Eric's Tip: I've diced the grilled angel food cake and turned this into an amazing layered trifle when making dessert for a large group!

Grilled Pineapple Sundae

SERVES 2

Ingredients

¼ pineapple, peeled & sliced

2 cups vanilla ice cream

¼ cup whipped cream

¼ cup sliced almonds

Directions

1. Place the Grill Plate on the Power Smokeless Grill and preheat the Grill to 390° F.

2. Place pineapple on Grill and grill until tender. Let cool, then chop.

3. Scoop ice cream into 2 serving dishes. Immediately before serving, top with pineapple, whipped cream, and sliced almonds.

Eric's Tip: You can also make an awesome dessert "salsa" by adding chopped strawberries and fresh mint.

Brioche French Toast

SERVES 6

Ingredients

10 eggs

¾ cup half & half

2 tsp. cinnamon

1 tsp. almond extract

¼ cup maple syrup, to serve

1 loaf brioche bread, thickly sliced

1 stick butter

Directions

1. In a bowl beat the eggs. Mix in half and half, cinnamon, and almond extract.

2. Soak bread in the egg batter for 5 mins.

3. Place the Griddle Plate on the Power Smokeless Grill and preheat the Grill to 350° F.

4. Place French toast slices on the Griddle and cook on each side until toasted and charred. Repeat until all slices are cooked.

5. Serve with maple syrup and butter.

Griddle Recipe

Grilled Apple Bowls & Vanilla Ice Cream

SERVES 4

Ingredients

Simple Syrup

1 cup sugar

1 cup water

1 cinnamon stick

---

2 apples, large

2 cups vanilla ice cream

½ cup caramel sauce

½ cup chopped pecans

Directions

1. **Simple syrup:** in a saucepan, bring the sugar, water, and cinnamon stick to a boil. Set aside.

2. Cut the apples in half and core with a melon baller. Add to the hot simple syrup.

3. Place the Grill Plate on the Power Smokeless Grill and preheat the Grill to 350° F.

4. Arrange apples on the Power Grill, cut side down. Grill for 3 mins. Flip and continue grilling until tender. Baste with simple syrup.

5. Top the apples with ice cream, caramel sauce, and chopped pecans immediately before serving.

Eric's Tip: These apples can also be made in advance. After grilling, cool in the refrigerator. When you are ready to serve, warm up in the microwave.

SERVES 2

Sweet Potato Pancakes

Ingredients

Wet

¾ cup sweet potato, cooked & pureed

2 eggs

1 cup buttermilk

3 tbsp. butter, melted, for batter

Dry

1 cup flour

2 tsp. baking powder

½ tsp. salt

½ tsp. cinnamon

¼ tsp. nutmeg

1 tbsp. brown sugar

2 tbsp. butter, for cooking

walnut or pecan syrup, for serving

sliced bananas, for serving

Directions

1. Mix the wet ingredients together and set aside.

2. Mix all dry ingredients together.

3. Make a well in the center and pour wet ingredients over dry ingredients. Gently fold together until combined.

4. Place the Griddle Plate on the Power Smokeless Grill and preheat the Grill to 350° F.

5. Melt 2 tbsp. butter on Griddle.

6. Dollop batter and cook pancakes until bubbles appear, flip, and continue cooking until done.

7. Serve with walnut or pecan syrup and bananas.

Griddle Recipe

French Toast Sundae

Ingredients

2 cups half & half

6 eggs

1 tsp. vanilla extract

1 tsp. salt

2 tbsp. cinnamon

1 loaf challah bread, sliced into 1-in. pieces

2 tbsp. butter, melted

vanilla ice cream, for serving

chopped walnuts, for serving

maple syrup, for serving

whipped cream, for serving

Directions

1. Place the Griddle Plate on the Power Smokeless Grill and preheat the Grill to 350° F.

2. In a large bowl, combine the half and half, eggs, vanilla, salt, and cinnamon. Whisk to combine.

3. Quickly submerge challah slices fully into the egg mixture.

4. Brush the Griddle with butter. Place the challah onto the Griddle. Cook until golden brown, about 2-3 mins. per side.

5. To serve, cut two pieces of French toast in half and arrange in a dish or bowl.

6. Top with vanilla ice cream and some chopped walnuts.

7. Drizzle with maple syrup and garnish with whipped cream before serving.

Griddle Recipe

INDEX